A STRAIGHTFORWARD GUIDE
TO
THE RIGHTS OF THE PRIVATE TENANT

ROGER SPROSTON

STRAIGHTFORWARD PUBLISHING
WWW.STRAIGHTFORWARDCO.CO.UK

Straightforward Publishing

© Roger Sproston 2019

ISBN

978-1-84716-917-4

Printed by 4edge Press www.4edge.co.uk

Cover design by BW Studio Derby

The information in this book was correct at the time of going to print. The author and publishers cannot be held liable for any errors or omissions within or for any changes in law since publication.

CONTENTS

Glossary of terms

Appendix 1 – Useful addresses

Appendix 2-Sample Assured Shorthold Tenancy Agreement (England and Wales)

Sample Section 21 Notice Requiring possession (FORM 6A)

Index

**

INTRODUCTION

This latest edition of A Straightforward Guide to the Rights of the Private Tenant, **2019**, substantially updates the previous edition by introducing more detailed information concerning the law, landlords obligations and tenants rights and obligations. A new chapter (2) dealing with people with disabilities and access to private housing has also been introduced

More and more people, in the next few years, due to factors such as inability to access finance to purchase a house, due to high costs of housing, changes in the housing benefit system and homelessness legislation will become reliant on the private sector. The private sector is rapidly expanding, because of a combination of these factors and rents are on the increase, in particular in London and the South East. In their recent report, Generation Rent, A Society Divided the Halifax states that the private rented sector is now at its highest level since the early 1990's. In 2018-2019 there are an estimated 22 million households in England and Wales living in private accommodation.

With no prospect of buying, more and more people will populate the private market over the coming years. Correspondingly, many more people have become landlords, particularly since 1988, and many more are set to become landlords, although the banks and government are making it that much harder through economic sanctions. It is the case, unfortunately, that this expansion introduces a lot of inexperienced people into the field. If an agent is used in the letting of property then there is (usually) no problem, although that is not a given. However, when the property is directly managed then issues can arise that can lead to conflict.

The response of the government to the rapid rise in private tenants and the corresponding problems of insecurity of tenure and sub-standard properties has been to tighten up the law regulating the sector.

Rogue Landlord Database, Banning Orders and Guidance Measures for Local Authorities to Tackle Substandard Practice

The government has released a range of new measures and guidance for local authorities that aim to tackle rogue landlords and letting agents in the private rental sector. The new measures come as part of the government's wider crackdown on substandard practice by landlords and letting agents, including a new database of rogue landlords and letting agents coming into force.

Subsequently, local authorities have also been provided with a wider range of guidelines and powers on banning orders, civil penalties and rent repayment orders.

The key guidelines and powers being introduced are as follows:

Database of Rogue Landlords and Property Agents

Landlords who are found to be renting out substandard properties will now face tougher consequences, with the introduction of a national database of rogue landlords and letting agents. The new database will include landlords and letting agents convicted of a range of housing and immigration offences, alongside other measures including:

- Unlawful eviction
- Breach of gas & fire safety measures
- Leasing overcrowded properties

Local councils will also be able to share information concerning rogue landlords and the specific offences committed, allowing local authorities to keep track off or take further action with those who have a poor track record.

Banning orders for landlords and property agents

Working in tandem with the new rogue landlord database, the banning order for rogue landlords and property agents under the Housing and Planning Act 2016 has provided local authorities with new powers to seek banning orders where the landlord or property agent has flouted their legal obligations or rented out substandard accommodation.

The updated guidance released aims to act as a comprehensive guide for local authorities when enforcing these powers.

Civil Penalties under the Housing and Planning Act

The government has also published updated guidance on civil penalties, which aims to help local authorities use their powers on imposing civil penalties as an alternative to prosecution.

The Housing and Planning Act 2016 gives local authorities powers to impose a civil penalty of up to £30,000 for a range of offences under the Housing and Planning Act 2004.

The updated guidance released today aims to reflect a civil penalty can be imposed for a breach of a banning order under the Housing and Planning Act 2016.

Rent Repayment Orders under the Housing and Planning Act

This extended guidance aims to help local authorities in using their powers to seek a rent repayment order against private sector landlords. The Housing and Planning Act 2016 extended rent repayment orders to cover illegal evictions and breaches of banning orders as well as a range of other offences.

In addition to the above, there are new Acts banning tenants fees and also restricting deposits along with other measures, all covered in this book.

14

Private lettings and Selective licensing

Where selective licensing applies, unlike the other forms of licensing which relate to HMOs (Housing in Multiple Occupation, (see chapter on Repairing obligations for more details on HMO's) then normally all houses within the private rented sector for that area must be licensed, except where they require to be licensed as HMOs. Non licensable HMOs must be licensed under Selective Licensing. "House" means a building or part of a building consisting of one or more dwellings. For those purposes "dwelling" means a building or part of a building occupied or intended to be occupied as a separate dwelling

Designation for Selective Licensing

Selective licensing is dependent on a designation by the local authority. A local authority may designate the whole of their district or part of their district, subject to selective licensing. An area may be designated for selective licensing either (i) if the area is (or is likely to be) an area of low housing demand **or** (ii) the area is experiencing a significant and persistent problem caused by anti social behaviour and some or all of the private sector landlords are failing to take action to combat the problem that it will be appropriate for them to take. A designation can last for five years. It can be renewed. There are prescribed publicity requirements for designations and the revocation of designations.

Properties to which Selective Licensing applies

Selective licenses are required for houses within the designated area where the whole of the house is occupied either under a single tenancy or licence

15

or under two or more tenancies or licences in respect of different dwellings contained in it.

Are there any exemptions?

A tenancy or licence is exempt from the selective licensing if it is granted by a registered social landlord.

The following tenancies/licences are also exempt where:

- a prohibition order is in force
- business tenancies
- licensed premises (for liquor licensing purposes)
- agricultural tenancies
- the property is managed/controlled by a local housing authority or public body
- the building is regulated under other legislation (e.g. care homes)
- the building is occupied by students controlled/managed by a University/College (who subscribe to an Approved Code of Practice)
- the occupier is a Member Of The Family of the landlord/licensor who himself holds under a lease of the property for a minimum of 21 years
- holiday lets
- the occupier shares any amenity (i.e. a toilet bathroom kitchen or living room) with the landlord/licensor or a Member Of The Family of the landlord/licensor

Temporary exemptions

if the landlord is taking steps to change the situation so that the property will no longer need to be licensed.

Differences between Selective Licensing and HMO Licensing

Generally, the same rules apply when granting a Selective Licence as with an HMO licence. The main differences are:-

- It is mandatory to take up references for a prospective tenant before letting a property subject to Selective Licensing.

- Unlike HMOs the licence authority does not have to consider suitability for letting or amenity standards when granting a selective licence. However, the licence holder must still be a fit and proper person.

Private landlords and new scheme to provide tenancies for the homeless-Homelessness Reduction Act 2017

As part of the Homeless Reduction Act discussed above the UK Government has announced a new £20 million fund to help people without a home get into the private rented sector. The fund aims to get councils to put in place vital new schemes so support the homeless into their own tenancies and will initially help up to 9,000 people but private landlords are also a part of the plan. This could involve councils providing financial support to help those to access or maintain their tenancies, such as paying deposits for the tenancy or rent payments. Alternatively, some schemes may involve the council managing the property on the landlord's behalf.

17

The fund is modelled on evidence provided from the successful programme run by leading homelessness charity Crisis which supported schemes to help homeless people into thousands of private rental tenancies.

The new fund's launch comes as patients, prisoners and jobseekers at risk of homelessness must now be referred to their local housing authority under key legislation. The duty to refer is a core part of the Homelessness Reduction Act 2017 and places new responsibilities on key public bodies such as prisons, Job centres and NHS Trusts to ensure those at risk get the help they need. Refer to the chapter on public sector housing for more detail on the Homeless Reduction Act 2017

Local authorities will have to bid for a portion of the £20 million available in the fund to provide financial support to help those in need access or maintain their tenancies.

The overall aim of this book is to ensure that all are clear about the law and practice of letting and residing in, private sector tenanted property. The book covers the finding of property and the role of letting agents, detailed information on specific tenancies, payments of rent and benefits and repairing obligations. Issues such as unlawful eviction and harassment are covered, as are public sector tenancies plus tenancies in Scotland. There is a section on the processes involved in regaining possession of a home for breach of tenancy.

The various notices used when going to court, and other forms associated with landlord and tenant can be obtained from the county courts. accessed and all the necessary forms required in relation to housing matters can be downloaded from:

www.gov.uk/government/organisations/hm-courts-and-tribunals-servicebe The court service website also gives a lot of valuable information in relation to housing.

The main aim of this book is to inform the would-be tenant, or the landlord, about their rights and obligations and covers all areas in depth. It is to be hoped that an invaluable insight is gained and that both landlord and tenant can operate more effectively.

Finally, this book is relevant to England and Wales, although there are slight differences in Wales concerning tenancies. For example every private landlord of a 'domestic tenancy' in Wales should be registered with the Rent Smart Wales scheme. This includes landlords of assured, assured shorthold and regulated tenancies. In addition, landlords who self-manage those tenancies, or agents who have been appointed by the landlord, must have a licence..For more information concerning Wales go to:

sheltercymru.org.uk/get-advice/renting/private-tenants-rights/
For Northern Ireland shelterni.org/
Scotland scotland.shelter.org.uk

**

Ch. 1

Private Tenants-Finding A Property

Letting Agents

One of the first places a prospective private tenant will look to rent a property is a lettings agent. It is important to know what the rules are governing agents as, particularly since the rise in demand for private properties, agents have started to use unscrupulous methods to extract more money from tenants and landlords, but particularly tenants,

An amendment to the Enterprise and Regulatory Reform Act 2013 enabled the Government to require agents to sign up to a redress scheme. The Redress Scheme for Lettings Agency Work and Property Management Work (Requirement to Belong to a Scheme etc) (England) Order 2014 made membership of a scheme a legal requirement with effect from 1 October 2014. There are also moves in 2019 to introduce a further tenants redress scheme.

The Government also amended the Consumer Rights Act 2015 to require letting agents to publish a full tariff of their fees. As mentioned previously, the charging of fees to tenants will be outlawed. This is scheduled to to come into effect in June 2019 along with new rules covering deposits. Deposits will be limited to five weeks, where annual rent is below £50,000 with new, stricter rules on holding deposits. The new rules will apply to all tenancies signed after 01 June.

Online lettings agents

The rise of online lettings agents has been rapid and they now account for 3.5% of the market. The attractions are obvious, the costs. One of the biggest online property agents, EasyProperty.com offers 'pick and mix' services ranging from £10 a week for adverts on Right Move, Prime Location and Zoopla to 3% commission for full property management. For tenant finding with all the frills, such as hosted viewings and professional photos, in the total bill would be £445. This equates to less than half the commission charged by high-street agents. Another agent, Purplebricks.com is also very competitive.

Typically a (good) letting agent will take responsibility for::

1   Transferring the utility bills and the council tax into the name of the tenant. Sign agreements and take up references.

2   Paying for repairs, although an agent will only normally do this if rent is being paid directly to them and they can make appropriate deductions.

3   Chasing rent arrears.

4   Serving notices of intent to seek possession if the landlord instructs them to do so. An agent cannot commence court proceedings except through a solicitor.

5   Visiting the property at regular intervals and check that the tenants are not causing any damage.

6   Dealing with neighbour complaints.

7   Banking rental receipts if the landlord is abroad

8   Dealing with housing benefit departments if necessary. The extent to which agents actually do any or all of the above really depends on the calibre of the agent. It also depends on the type of agreement you have with the agent.

Immigration Act 2014 and checking eligibility to rent

In October 2014, the Immigration Act 2014 came into force which puts the responsibility on landlords to vet their tenants, or prospective tenants to check to see if they have a right to be in the country (the obligation came into force in February 2016). Only when this is verified can a letting go ahead. More information about the Right to Rent checks can be obtained from www.gov.uk.

Discrimination against tenants on housing benefits

There is a significant push to ensure that tenants on housing benefits are not discriminated against. From April 2019, Rightmove and Zoopla will both take down listings that say NO DSS (the now defunct Department of Social Security). Others are likely to follow suit.

Company lets

Where the tenant is a company rather than an individual, the tenancy agreement will be similar to an assured shorthold but will not be bound by the six-month rule (see chapter eight for details of assured shorthold tenancies). Company lets can be from any length of time, from a week to several years, or as long as you like.

The major difference between contracts and standard assured shorthold agreements is that the contract will be tailored to individual needs, and the agreement is bound by the provisions of contract law. Company tenancies are bound by the provisions of contract law and not by the Housing Acts.

Short-lets

Generally speaking, short-lets are only applicable in large cities where there is a substantial shifting population. Business executives on temporary relocation, actors and others involved in television production or film work, contract workers and visiting academics are examples of people who might require a short-let.

From a landlord's point of view, short-lets are an excellent idea if they have to vacate your own home for seven or eight months, say, and do not want to leave it empty.

Short-let tenants provide useful extra income as well as keeping an eye on the place. Or if you are buying a new property and have not yet sold the old one, it can make good business sense to let it to a short-let tenant.

Short-let tenants are, usually, from a landlord's point of view, excellent blue-chip occupants. They are busy professionals, high earners, out all day and used to high standards. As the rent is paid by the company there is no worry for the landlord on this score either. A major plus of short-lets is that they command between 20-50 percent more rent than the optimum market rent for that type of property.

The one downside of short-lets is that no agency can guarantee permanent occupancy.

Student lets

Many mainstream letting agencies will not consider students and a lot of landlords similarly are not keen. There is the perception that students will not look after a home and tend to live a lifestyle guaranteed to increase the wear and tear on a property. However, a number of specialist companies have grown up which concentrate solely on students. Although students quite often want property for only eight or nine months, agencies that deal with students make them sign for a whole year. Rent is guaranteed by confirmation that the student is a genuine student with references from parents, who act as guarantors.

Holiday lets

Before the Housing Act 1988 became law, many landlords advertised their properties as holiday lets to bypass the then rules regarding security of tenure. Strictly speaking, a holiday let is a property let for no more than a month to any one tenant. If the same tenant renews for another month then the landlord is breaking the law. Nowadays, holiday lets must be just that; let for a genuine holiday. If you have a flat or cottage that you wish to let for holiday purposes, whether or not you live in it yourself for part of the year, you are entering into a quite different agreement with the tenant. Holiday lets are not covered by the Housing Act. The contract is finalised by exchange of letters with the tenant where they place a deposit and the owner confirms the booking. If the let is not for a genuine holiday you may have problems in evicting the tenant.

Generally speaking, certain services must be provided for the let to be deemed a holiday let. Cleaning services and changes of bed linen are essential. The amount paid by the holiday-maker will usually include utilities but would exclude use of the telephone, fax machine etc.

Bedsits

Bedsitting rooms are usually difficult to let and can cause problems. There are numerous regulations to adhere to. Houses in Multiple Occupation regulations are quite strict.

The Housing Act 2004 has introduced new tougher regulations for HMOs. If a landlord is letting out property in a block with more than three unrelated dwellings then a licence will be needed from the local authority before lettings can take place. (see chapter on repairs for more details about HMO's)

Landlords taking in a lodger

One way of finding accommodation is to approach people, through websites listed below, who wish to take in a lodger. the following are the main points to consider:

- Under the current Rent a Room Scheme a person can earn rental income of up to £7,500 a year (£625 a month from 2018/19) from a furnished room in their house, without having to pay tax on it.

- Prospective Landlords can find lodgers using listings websites such as uk.easyroommate.com and mondaytofriday.com and spareroom.co.uk or fivenights.com (as their names suggest, the last two sites specialise in lodgers who need only weekday accommodation).

- A lodger may be a friend or relation; in other cases, its important to vet anyone thoroughly before they move in. Experian, the credit reference agency, offers a tenants' screening service, under which a landlord can check a prospective tenant's identity, references and ability to pay the rent. The service costs from £15-£25. The prospective tenant must give permission for his or her detail to be shared with you.

- A prospective landlord has certain responsibilities for example, they need to ensure that their gas appliances have been tested for safety. For more details go to gassaferegister.co.uk

- A prospective landlord may prefer to dispense with a legal agreement with your lodger but, if they prefer a more formal relationship they can download the necessary documentation from lawpack.co.uk The agreement should set out every detail of how the arrangement will work, including rent, what parts of the house the lodger can use, whether guests can stay overnight, and on what basis the arrangement can be terminated.

- If the landlord shares their kitchen, bathroom or living room with a lodger, you can evict this person at any time – giving reasonable notice. This is normally 28 days. Under the law, the lodger is viewed as an "excluded occupier" rather than as a tenant. For more on this, see the government website: gov.uk/rent-room-in-your-home/the-rent-a-room-scheme

- A prospective landlord should notify their home and contents insurer and their mortgage lender before taking in a lodger. If they are a tenant themselves, subletting a room in this way could give rise to problems: they should check their own tenancy agreement.

- The Airbnb website enables people to let a room – or whole property – hotel-style, on an ad hoc basis. landlords can charge considerably higher rates per night than they would charge a lodger, and there is greater flexibility as they may choose to let a room for only a few weeks a year. Airbnb hosts with stylish properties in London can charge £150-plus a night for large bedroom with en suite, but guests expect standards commensurate with prices.

- It is free to advertise rooms on airbnb.co.uk. The company sends a photographer to take pictures for your listing. Hosts use the Airbnb site's software to manage bookings, and they pay commission of 3per cent on each accepted reservation. Similar websites include Wimdu. However, Revenue & Customs could consider that regular hosts are running a business, so check before assuming that earnings qualify for the Rent a Room Scheme.

Letting through Airbnb

Over the last few years, landlords have increasingly turned to companies like Airbnb to let their properties. What started out as a good concept has, as usual been ruined by those looking for a quick return, Airbnb started out as a web based company offering an alternative to hotels, particularly in the overpriced capitals of the world. Landlords now see that there is a profit to be made by allowing a succession of short term tenants to stay in their properties. However, problems have arisen and the courts have found that for landlords with leasehold property to allow their properties to be used by a succession of short term tenants is actually a breach of the lease.

Deposits-Tenancy Deposit Protection Scheme

The Tenancy Deposit Protection Scheme was introduced to protect all deposits paid to landlords (except landlords of common law tenancies such as company lets) after 6th April 2007. After this date, landlords and/or agents must use a government authorised scheme to protect deposits. The need for such a scheme has arisen because of the historical problem with deposits. (As mentioned deposits will be limited to five weeks, where annual rent is below £50,000 with new, stricter rules on holding deposits. The new rules will apply to all tenancies signed after 01 June). The scheme works as below.

Moving into a property

At the beginning of a new tenancy agreement, the tenant will pay a deposit to the landlord or agent as usual. Within 14 days the landlord is required to give the tenant details of how the deposit is going to be protected including:

- the contact details of the tenancy deposit scheme
- the contact details of landlord or agent
- how to apply for the release of the deposit
- what to do if there is a dispute about the deposit

There are three tenancy deposit schemes that a landlord can opt for:

Tenancy Deposit Solutions Ltd

www.mydeposits.co.uk

info@mydeposits.co.uk

The Tenancy Deposit Scheme

www.tds.gb.com

0845 226 7837

The Deposit Protection Service

www.depositprotection.com

0870 707 1 707

The schemes above fall into two categories, insurance based schemes and custodial schemes.

Custodial Scheme

- The tenant pays the deposit to the landlord
- The landlord pays the deposit into the scheme
- Within 14 days of receiving the deposit, the landlord must give the tenant prescribed information
- A the end of the tenancy, if the landlord and tenant have agreed how much of the deposit is to be returned, they will tell the scheme which returns the deposit, divided in the way agreed by the parties.
- If there is a dispute, the scheme will hold the disputed amount until the dispute resolution service or courts decide what is fair
- The interest accrued by deposits in the scheme will be used to pay for the running of the scheme and any surplus will be used to offer interest to the tenant, or landlord if the tenant isn't entitled to it.

Insurance based schemes

- The tenant pays the deposit to the landlord
- The landlord retains the deposit and pays a premium to the insurer (this is the key difference between the two schemes)
- Within 14 days of receiving a deposit the landlord must give the tenant prescribed information.
- At the end of the tenancy if the landlord and tenant agree how the deposit is to be divided or otherwise then the landlord will return the amount agreed
- If there is a dispute, the landlord must hand over the disputed amount to the scheme.
- If for any reason the landlord fails to comply, the insurance arrangements will ensure the return of the deposit to the tenant if they are entitled to it.

If a landlord or agent hasn't protected a deposit with one of the above then the tenant can apply to the local county court for an order for the landlord either to protect the deposit or repay it.

The Deregulation Act 2015

Since 6 April 2007, it has been mandatory for a landlord to ensure that a tenant's deposit that has been paid in respect of an assured shorthold tenancy (AST) is protected within a Tenancy Deposit Scheme. The Deregulation Act now extends the requirement to protect a deposit to AST's created before 6 April 2007 in certain circumstances. Landlords are now required to protect their deposits within a scheme and serve the prescribed information relating to the deposit on the tenant. If a landlord fails to do this then it is prevented from recovering possession of the property from the tenant and is potentially liable for financial penalties.

Rental guarantees

The landlord is always advised to obtain a guarantor if there is any potential uncertainty as to payment of rent. One example is where the tenant is on benefits. The guarantor will be expected to assume responsibility for the rent if the tenant ceases to pay at any time during the term of the tenancy.

**

Ch. 2

Private Housing For the Disabled

This chapter covers Disabled Housing in England. For housing rights and disabled in Wales, Scotland and Northern Ireland go to:

https://scotland.shelter.org.uk (Scotland)

https://www.housingadviceni.org/accessible-housing (Ireland)

https://sheltercymru.org.uk (Wales)

In most parts of the country now, there are relatively few social properties available, and increasing numbers of people are renting from private landlords, which brings with it different problems, which we cover below. Renting from a private landlord is different to renting from a social housing provider in several ways: – There are lots of homes available to rent privately (depending where you live of course). That gives you a good chance of finding a home where you want to live, e.g. near to your family and friends, schools, work, or health facilities. In addition, you will usually be able to find a property more quickly: this is very helpful if you need to move to a new area to start a course or a job, or you need a place temporarily while you wait for social housing or save up to buy a property.

If you are homeless, the council may well place you in private rented property – at least temporarily, or even permanently (although this will be governed by supply and demand in an area..

In the private sector you should be aware that: – The rent is likely to be higher than in the social rented sector. – If you are entitled to either Housing Benefit or the housing element of Universal Credit, you can use this to pay your rent; however, it may not cover the full cost. It can be more difficult (but may be possible) to make changes to a private rented property so that it meets your needs. There is less 'security of tenure' – in other words, it is easier for your landlord to ask you to move out, even if you have been a good tenant.

Can you rent specialist housing for older people privately?

Retirement living properties, which usually have above-average accessibility and may benefit from on-site support and care, are an option for disabled people aged 55 and over. Normally you would apply via your council to either rent (social rent) or buy a leasehold property. However, there is also an emerging private rent market for these properties, either from individuals who own them, or from providers themselves.

Despite the number of properties available to rent at any time, it can be challenging to find somewhere that meets your access requirements – or even to find out whether a property does or does not meet your access requirements. This is especially true if you need somewhere that is fully wheelchair-accessible. Many private landlords and letting agencies advertise available properties online, using the rental pages of websites such as Zoopla and Rightmove. However, these websites don't currently allow you to search for accessible properties or particular access features. Rightmove can filter searches for bungalows, but these may or may not be fully accessible.

It can be a good idea to contact letting agencies that operate in the area you want to live and explain your access requirements to them. You could search for an Association of Residential Lettings Agents (ARLA) Propertymark Protected letting agent. They may be able to identify potential properties for you and let you know as soon as they become available – though you may need to build this relationship and check in with them regularly. You should also be aware that letting agencies' loyalties ultimately lie with the landlord, so do not expect them to give you completely impartial advice.

Lettings agents must by law make their application processes (e.g. any forms you need to complete) accessible to you.

There are also some companies who specialise in finding accessible properties –again, check that they are registered with ARLA. In some areas, there are 'social' (not for profit) lettings agencies and the criteria for using these agencies varies. For example, sometimes you need to be homeless and referred by the council –but it is worth finding out. Your council will be able to advise.

You should also speak to the housing options team at your council if you have not already done so. If you are at risk of homelessness or your current property is so unsuitable for your needs that you could be described as effectively homeless, they should help you consider your housing options in both the social and private rented sector. They may be able to refer you to a social letting agency or give you a list of private letting agencies operating in your area. Even if your housing needs are not so urgent, they may still be able to give you some pointers on trying to find an adapted or accessible property locally, and/or accessing funding locally to help meet the cost of adaptations. Arrange to view any properties that sound promising to see if they actually work for you.

The lettings process

Pre-tenancy checks

As we have discussed in the previous chapter, before you can rent a property, you will need to show your passport or another document that demonstrates you have a right to rent in the UK. The landlord or letting agency want to be sure you will be a good tenant. There are various ways of doing this, and some are more flexible than others: – You may be asked for references from current or previous landlords, employers, or someone else who can vouch that you will be a good tenant. – You will probably be asked for evidence that you can afford the rent, e.g. benefit letters, payslips/work contracts, bank statements (make sure you hide the account number). – They will usually want to run a credit check. – Alternatively, you may be able to use a 'guarantor' – this is someone who signs to say they are willing to pay the rent if you do not, and is usually a family member who will need to meet certain financial criteria themselves. You can find more detailed advice on the Citizens Advice website.

Payments at the start of the tenancy

You will generally need to pay your rent monthly and in advance. This means you will need to pay a month's rent upfront. At the start of the tenancy, you will also often need to pay the landlord a deposit. This is to protect them against the risk of you damaging the property and/or leaving without paying the rent. The landlord must put this in one of three government-backed 'tenancy deposit schemes' within 30 days. These schemes will make sure you get all your deposit back at the end of the tenancy, provided you keep to your side of the tenancy agreement.

It is possible that you will be able to get help with the payments at the start of a tenancy, through a rent deposit, bond and guarantee scheme run by a council, housing association or charity. Most of these are given to people who are homeless and/or 'vulnerable', so you will need to be in urgent housing need. You could check Crisis's Help to Rent database to see if there are any schemes in your area, though you will need to check with the local scheme to find out if you are eligible.

How to rent guide

It is now law for your landlord (or letting agent) to hand you a copy of the How to rent guide at the start of the tenancy. This outlines what you and your landlord should expect from each other. It contains important information, such as: – questions to ask once you have found a property – how to navigate the ending of your tenancy – what to do if things go wrong.

My rights and responsibilities as a tenant

The tenancy

The tenancy is the contract between you ('the tenant') and the person who owns the property ('the landlord'), which allows you to live in it. The tenancy sets out the rights and responsibilities of both the tenant and the landlord. Tenants have rights, but also have responsibilities: most notably, to pay your rent on time and to keep the property in a reasonable condition. The tenancy should state the amount of rent due, when it should be paid and how long the contract lasts.

Most private tenants have an 'assured shorthold tenancy'. Since housing law has changed over time, if your tenancy started before February 1997, you should check what kind of tenancy you have. It should say on the tenancy document you have from your landlord. You may have an assured or protected tenancy, in which case you have slightly different rights. See the Citizens Advice website for more details on this. The UK Government has produced a model tenancy agreement. Landlords don't have to use it but it is free to use, so you could suggest this (or compare and check against the tenancy agreement you are issued with). Your tenancy may also include an 'inventory' – this lists any furniture and fittings that are provided with the property and the condition they are in at the start of the tenancy. You should agree this carefully at the outset with the landlord/letting agency. If you ask your landlord to provide the tenancy document in a version that is accessible to you (e.g. braille, audio, large print, easy read, another language) they must (under the Equality Act 2010) do so. Everyone should have the opportunity to ask questions about their tenancy at sign-up, whatever their access and communication needs.

Making adaptations to a property

If you are finding it difficult to access basic facilities in your home or feel unsafe getting around your property, you may benefit from a home adaptation. Aids and adaptations are not only for people with reduced mobility; they may also help people with sensory impairments, dementia or mental health conditions. They could range from a small piece of equipment or technology right through to a major structural change, with the aim of improving your independence, confidence and privacy. If you live in a block of flats with some communal facilities, your landlord can make 'reasonable adjustments' to improve access to and within communal areas.

If equipment or an adaptation costs less than £1,000, your council (or in some cases the NHS) should provide this for free. You will need to get the permission of your landlord to make a change to your property, but, under the Equality Act 2010, they cannot refuse unless they have 'reasonable grounds' for doing so. Examples of things to look at to decide whether your landlord has a good reason for refusing an adaptation include: > the type and length of the letting > your ability to pay for the improvement > how easy it is to make the adaptations (and how easy it would be to undo them), and > the extent of any disruption and effect on other occupiers. – If the adaptation costs more than £1,000, you will need to apply for a Disabled Facilities Grant (DFG) from your local housing authority. DFGs are generally means-tested but the council cannot refuse this solely because you are a private rented tenant, if you and your landlord are willing to confirm that you plan to stay in the property for the next five years. This is confirmed by the tenant and owner submitting a 'tenant's certificate' and an 'owner's certificate' respectively.

There are exceptions where the landlord can refuse to make the improvements, particularly if you are renting a room in a shared house, for example if: – the property you are renting has been the main home of the landlord – you share facilities such as the kitchen, bathroom or living room (the exception does not apply when you only share access to the property or storage areas) – the landlord or landlord's family member lives in the property, or – the property is not large enough to accommodate more than six lodgers or two separate households. At the moment, the Equality Act 2010 does not require the landlord to make structural changes to your property, or the 'common parts' of a block of flats.

Dealing with problems in your tenancy

Problems with heating, appliances and repairs

Your landlord has legal obligations to ensure that their property is safe for you to live in. If your health is negatively affected by the condition of the property, you may be within your rights to demand repairs to rectify the problem. Landlords are legally responsible for ensuring that: – the building's structure is sound, including external roofs, walls, windows and doors. – internal sanitation and plumbing is fully functional and safe, and that heating and hot water is properly maintained. – chimneys and other means of ventilation are safe and in good working order. – gas appliances are safely installed and maintained by a Gas Safe registered engineer, who must provide an annual gas safety check on appliances and flues: you should be given a copy of the gas safety record within 28 days of the check, all electrical goods and mains are safe, including fixtures and any equipment they supply with the property, fire safety regulations are followed, including installing smoke alarms, fire safe furniture and fittings, and providing access to escape routes: these need to be accessible to you. If you live in a House in Multiple Occupation (HMO),2 large properties are required to have a fire alarm system and extinguishers installed. HMOs must have a HMO Licence under UK law. To check that a HMO Licence is in place, you can contact your council. Failure of the landlord to comply may lead to their prosecution and/or imprisonment. If you think your landlord is failing on any of the above, you should complain to them (larger landlords or letting agencies should have a formal complaints procedure). Putting complaints in writing/email and keeping a copy can be helpful should you end up taking legal action.

Getting your deposit back when you move out

You should get your deposit back when you move out, but the landlord can make 'reasonable' deductions from this to cover unpaid rent, damage to the property, missing items (listed in the inventory) and/or cleaning costs. If you think your landlord is being unreasonable or they are refusing to give the deposit back, there are steps you can take. For example, the deposit protection scheme has a free Dispute Resolution Service. Shelter sets out the steps you should take in some detail on their website.

Making complaints

Many complaints can be solved by discussing the issue with your landlord in the first instance. If this fails, there are a number of ways you can make a formal complaint. Check if your landlord or letting agency has a complaints procedure. Make complaints by email or in writing (keeping a copy). Where disputes are unresolved, you could complain to a 'designated person', which might be your MP or local councillor, or contact your council for further advice. Your council's private sector licensing or enforcement team or, in the case of problems like pests, damp and leaks, their environmental health team may be able to help. Citizens Advice offer further advice on their website on complaining about your landlord.

Information about private renting

Shelter offers many online resources, including: – Housing advice – Contact a housing advisor. Citizens Advice also provides advice and guidance. The Tenants' Voice is the biggest tenant community in the UK, and has a website full of information about renting and getting advice related to your renting problems.

Finding an advocate

An advocate can help you express your views and stand up for your rights. Your council may fund an advocacy service in your area, so check with them. If you have a mental health condition, see Mind's website. If you have a cognitive impairment,

Citizens Advice has a dedicated webpage on taking action on discrimination in housing. If you think you have experienced discrimination, you can get help and advice from the Equality Advisory and Support Service.

Legal help

Legal aid (to help pay for legal presentation in civil cases) is not as readily available as it used to be. However, there are still particular circumstances in which you might be eligible to receive it, and there are some remaining sources of free legal advice. See Shelter's website. If you are at risk of harm, you must seek advice as soon as possible from your council's housing options team. You can find the website of your local council. It may also a good idea to get independent advice from Shelter or Citizens Advice. Other sources of support. Local or impairment-specific disability charities may be able to offer support. You could contact your local councillor or MP You can find out who they are by entering your postcode on the UK Government website or UK Parliament website. The Samaritans can provide emotional support and should be able to suggest sources of practical help and advocacy in your area. You don't need to be suicidal.

Your rights as an existing tenant

You have rights: – as a tenant, as set out in your tenancy agreement – as a disabled person, under the Equality Act 2010, and – as a human being, under the Human Rights Act 1998

Your rights as a disabled person

If you are disabled (the legal definition of 'disabled' is available on the UK Government website). Your social landlord has a duty under the Equality Act 2010 to make 'reasonable adjustments' or provide 'auxiliary aids and services' so that you can rent and live in a property. This might, for example, include: – providing written agreements in a way that is accessible to you, such as large print, braille, audio, easy read, or in a language other than English. – making changes so you can use any facilities and benefits

41

that come with the property in the same way as a non-disabled tenant, e.g. a wider parking space, or a ramp to access the common garden, and – holding the tenant panel meetings in a room with a hearing loop fitted so you can attend and participate. This does not necessarily mean that the landlord is required to make structural changes to your property

Your landlord only has a duty to make them if they are 'reasonable' – this will depend on: the length and type of tenancy you have; the cost of the adjustment (and the landlord's financial circumstances), and how effective the adjustment is likely to be. Your social landlord also has a duty under the Equality Act 2010 to change a policy or practice (including the term of a tenancy agreement) if it disadvantages you because you are disabled.

ADAPTING A HOME

What is a 'home adaptation'?

If you are finding it difficult to access basic facilities in your home or feel unsafe getting around your property, you may benefit from a home adaptation. Aids and adaptations aren't only for people with reduced mobility; they may also help people with sensory impairments, dementia or even mental health conditions. They could range from a small piece of equipment or technology right through to a major structural change, with the aim of improving your independence, confidence and privacy. Adaptations aren't just about physical access – they might, for example, include building a separate room for a child with autism who is not able to share with a sibling, or changing lighting and acoustics to reduce stress for a person living with dementia. For an adaptation to work, you need to make sure you have found the right solution for your individual needs and the property you live in.

It is important to understand the differences between 'equipment', 'minor adaptations' and 'major adaptations', as the process for accessing them and rules around funding differ for each.

Equipment

'Equipment' is generally portable and can be loaned for a period of time or taken by a person to another property. Examples might include: – a portable wheelchair ramp or raised toilet seat – adapted kitchen utensils and equipment – a hearing aid. Funding and access

Equipment is usually provided free of charge (or on some occasions with a small deposit, e.g. £20) if you are assessed as needing it by: – a trusted assessor (who might be an occupational therapist – or social worker) working for the local authority, or – a health professional (GP, hospital clinic, district nurse, community physiotherapist).

Minor adaptations

'Minor adaptions' are changes that are made to the home and typically cost up to £1,000. Examples might include: – a short ramp and/or some grab rails – a door-release intercom system – changes to lighting and paintwork for a person with dementia and/or low vision. Minor adaptations can be approved and funded by your local authority, following an occupational therapy assessment, as part of a care assessment by adult social care services.

Major adaptations

'Major adaptations' typically cost over £1,000 and require substantial or structural works to your home. Examples might include: – the installation of a wet floor shower – ramped access that requires the widening of external doorways – replacing kitchen units with adjustable worktops – building an extension on to the property and/or a ground floor bathroom.

Funding and access

Disabled Facilities Grants can help cover the costs of major adaptations, whether you own your property or rent. The Grant is often means-tested based on your income, your partner's income (if applicable) and your savings, so you may well need to pay towards the cost of the work. The Grant is not means-tested if you are applying on behalf of a child under 18. Some local authorities have abandoned means-testing altogether. To start the process, you need to request an assessment for your social care team. Your local or district council is responsible for administering the Grant, which can provide up to £30,000 of funding. You can apply for funding to help with the costs of home adaptations whether you own your home or rent it from either a social or private landlord.

If you rent from a housing association or you are a council tenant, you should find out first from them how to go about applying for a major adaptation. Some may direct you to the council to apply for a Disabled Facilities Grant for major adaptations, but almost all will want to arrange for and oversee the works to your home.

What is 'occupational therapy'?

Occupational therapy, often referred to as OT, is a healthcare profession that focuses on developing, recovering, or maintaining the daily living and working skills of people with physical, mental, or cognitive impairments. It is a good idea to start by speaking to an occupational therapist when you are thinking about equipment or adaptations. Occupational therapy services are available free of charge from the NHS or social services – if you do not already have an occupational therapist, the best thing to do is contact your council's adult social care team, or you could ask your GP to make a referral. You also have the option to use an independent occupational therapist: they will charge a fee, but they usually don't have waiting lists and can offer services that the state does not fund. You can find a private occupational therapist by searching on the Royal College of Occupational Therapists website.

In England, under the Care Act 2014, you are entitled to a Needs Assessment by your council's adult social care team. This should explore how home adaptations might improve your ability to carry out everyday tasks at home.

You may find that there is a long wait for an occupational therapist or a social work assessment. However, once they have assessed you as needing a piece of equipment, this should be provided by the local community equipment store (usually joint funded by health and social services).

The Independent Living Buyers' Guide is a good place to research possible solutions that might work for you. As the title suggests, it is geared more towards people who are willing and able to buy their own equipment, so not all items will be available free through the NHS or your council. There are lots of ways in which technology can be used to promote independent living

**

Ch. 3

The Law in a Nutshell

Explaining the law

As a tenant, or potential tenant, it is very important to understand the rights and obligations of both yourself and your landlord, exactly what can and what cannot be done once the tenancy agreement has been signed and you have moved into the property.

Some landlords think they can do exactly as they please, because the property belongs to them. Some tenants do not know any differently and therefore the landlord can, and often does, get away with breaking the law. However there is a very strong legal framework governing the relationship between landlord and tenant and it is important that you have a grasp of the key principles of the law.

In order to fully understand the law we should begin by looking at the main types of relationship between people and their homes.

The freehold and the lease

In law, there are two main types of ownership and occupation of property. These are: freehold and leasehold. These arrangements are very old indeed. In the section dealing with the relationship between leaseholder and freeholder, towards the end of this book, we will be discussing leasehold and freehold in more depth.

Freehold

If a person owns their property outright (usually with a mortgage) then they are a freeholder. The only claims to ownership over and above their own might be those of the building society or the bank, which lent them the money to buy the property. They will re-possess the property if the mortgage payments are not kept up with.

In certain situations though, the local authority (council) for an area can affect a person's right to do what they please with their home even if they are a freeholder. This will occur when planning powers are exercised, for example, in order to prevent the carrying out of alterations without consent.

The local authority for your area has many powers and we will be referring to these regularly.

Leasehold

If a person lives in a property owned by someone else and has a written agreement allowing them to occupy the flat or house for a period of time i.e., giving them permission to live in that property, then they will, in the main, have a lease and either be a leaseholder or a tenant of a landlord.

The main principle of a lease is that a person has been given permission by someone else to live in his or her property for a period of time. The person giving permission could be either the freeholder or another leaseholder. The tenancy agreement is one type of lease. If you have signed a tenancy agreement then you will have been given permission by a person to live in their property for a period of time.

The position of the tenant

The tenant will usually have an agreement for a shorter period of time than the typical leaseholder. Whereas the leaseholder will, for example, have an agreement for ninety-nine years, the tenant will have an agreement, which either runs from week to week or month to month (periodic tenancy) or is for a fixed term, for example, six-months or one-year. These arrangements are the most common types of agreement between the private landlord and tenant. The agreement itself will state whether it is a fixed term or periodic tenancy. If an agreement has not been issued it will be assumed to be a fixed-term tenancy.

Both periodic and fixed term tenants will usually pay a sum of rent regularly to a landlord in return for permission to live in the property (more about rent and service charges later)

The tenancy agreement

The tenancy agreement is the usual arrangement under which one person will live in a property owned by another. Before a tenant moves into a property he/she will have to sign a tenancy agreement drawn up by a landlord or landlord's agent. *A tenancy agreement is a contract between landlord and tenant.* It is important to realize that when you sign a tenancy agreement, you have signed a contract with another person, which governs the way in which you will live in their property.

The contract

Typically, any tenancy agreement will show the name and address of the landlord and will state the names of the tenant(s). The type of tenancy agreement that is signed should be clearly indicated. This could be, for example, a Rent Act protected tenancy, an assured tenancy or an assured shorthold tenancy. In the main, in the private sector, the agreement will be an assured shorthold.

Date of commencement of tenancy and rent payable

The date the tenancy began and the duration (fixed term or periodic) plus the amount of rent payable should be clearly shown, along with who is responsible for any other charges, such as water rates, council tax etc, and a description of the property you are living in.

In addition to the rent that must be paid there should be a clear indication of when a rent increase can be expected. This information is sometimes shown in other conditions of tenancy, which should be given to the tenant when they move into their home. The conditions of tenancy will set out landlords and tenants rights and obligations.

Services provided under the tenancy and service of notice

If services are provided, i.e., if a service charge is payable, this should be indicated in the agreement. The tenancy agreement should indicate clearly the address to which notices on the landlord can be served by the tenant, for example, because of repair problems or notice of leaving the property. The landlord has a legal requirement to indicate this.

Tenants obligations

The tenancy agreement will either be a basic document with the above information or will be more comprehensive. Either way, there will be a section beginning "the tenant agrees." Here the tenant will agree to move into the property, pay rent, use the property as an only home, not cause a nuisance to others, take responsibility for certain internal repairs, not sublet the property, i.e., create another tenancy, and various other things depending on the property. (The government is, at the moment, actively considering allowing tenants to sublet). It is important that when looking at a tenancy agreement it complies with legislation.

Landlords obligations

There should also be another section "the landlord agrees". Here, the landlord is contracting with the tenant to allow quiet enjoyment of the property. The landlord's repairing responsibilities are also usually outlined.

Ending a tenancy

Finally, there should be a section entitled "ending the tenancy" which will outline the ways in which landlord and tenant can end the agreement. The landlord can only end a fixed term assured shorthold tenancy by issuing a s21 notice (so called because it arises out of section 21 of the Housing Act 1988, as amended) two months prior to the end of the tenancy. Many landlords issued this notice at the outset of the tenancy. However, the Deregulation Act 2015 has effectively stopped this practice and states that the landlord cannot now service the notice until the tenant has been in occupation for at least four months. The tenant, after the expiry of the fixed term, can give one months notice to leave. One more point worth noting is that, if the landlord issues notice, in the required format, by text or email this is likely to be accepted as valid notice.

The landlord must serve a notice by using Form 6A for all tenancies created on or after October 1st 2015. This form must be used for all ASTs created on or after 1 October 2015 except for statutory periodic tenancies which have come into being on or after 1 October 2015 at the end of fixed term ASTs created before 1 October 2015.

See appendix for a sample Form 6A.

It is also in this section of the tenancy that the landlord should make reference to the "grounds for possession". Grounds for possession are circumstances where the landlord will apply to court for possession of his/her property. Some of these grounds relate to what is in the tenancy, i.e., the responsibility to pay rent and to not cause a nuisance. Other grounds do not relate to the contents of the tenancy directly, but more to the law governing that particular tenancy. The grounds for possession are very important, as they are used in any court case brought against the tenant. Unfortunately, they are not always indicated in the tenancy agreement. As they are so important they are summarized later on in the next chapter.

It must be said at this point that many residential tenancies are very light on spelling out landlord's responsibilities. For example, repairing responsibilities are landlords obligations under law. This book deals with these obligations, and also other important areas. However, many landlords will seek to use only the most basic document in order to conceal legal obligations.

This is one of the main reasons for this book. It is essential that those who intend to let property for profit are able to manage professionally and set high standards as a private landlord. This is because the sector has been beset by rogues in the past. Correspondingly, as a tenant you need to know your rights very clearly and need to know how to enforce them.

The responsibility of the landlord to provide a rent book

If the tenant is a weekly periodic tenant the landlord must provide him/her with a rent book and commits a criminal offence if he/she does not do so. This is outlined in the Landlord and Tenant Act 1985 sections 4 - 7. Under this Act any tenant can ask in writing the name and address of the landlord. The landlord must reply within twenty-one days of asking. As most tenancies nowadays are fixed term assured shortholds then it is not strictly necessary to provide a tenant with a rent book.. However, for the purposes of efficiency, and your own records, it is always useful to have a rent book and sign it each time rent is collected or a standing order is paid.

Overcrowding

It is important to understand, when signing a tenancy agreement, that it is not permitted to allow the premises to become overcrowded, i.e., to allow more people than was originally intended, (which is outlined in the agreement) to live in the property. If a tenant does, then the landlord can take action to evict.

Different types of tenancy agreement

The protected tenancy - the meaning of the term

As a basic guide, if a person is a private tenant and signed their current agreement with a landlord before 15th January 1989 then they will, in most cases, be a protected tenant with all the rights relating to protection of tenure, which are considerable. Protection is provided under the 1977 Rent Act.

In practice, there are not many protected tenancies left and the tenant will usually be signing an assured shorthold tenancy.

The assured shorthold tenancy - what it means

If the tenant entered into an agreement with a landlord after 15th January 1989 then they will, in most cases, be an assured tenant. We will discuss assured tenancies in more depth in chapter three. In brief, there are various types of assured tenancy. The assured shorthold is usually a fixed term version of the assured tenancy and enables the landlord to recover their property after six months and to vary the rent after this time. *It is this tenancy that a private tenant will be signing.*

Other types of agreement

In addition to the above tenancy agreements, there are other types of agreement sometimes used in privately rented property. One of these is the company let, as we discussed in the last chapter, and another is the license agreement. The person signing such an agreement is called a licensee. Licenses will only apply in special circumstances where the licensee cannot be given sole occupation of his home and therefore can only stay for a short period with minimum rights.

**

Ch. 4

More About Assured Tenants

The assured tenant

As we discussed in Chapter two, all tenancies, (with the exceptions detailed entered into after 15th January 1989), are known as assured tenancies. An assured shorthold, which is the most common form of tenancy used by the landlord nowadays, is one type of assured tenancy, and is for a fixed term of six months minimum and can be brought to an end with two months notice by serving a section 21 (of the Housing Act 1988) notice.

For Assured shorthold tenancies beginning after October 1st 2015, a Form 6A must be used. it is possible to use form 6A for tenancies issued before that date although not necessary

As stated earlier, as a result of the passage of the 2015 Deregulation Act, the landlord cannot serve the notice until the tenant has been in occupation for four months (at least).

It is important to note that all tenancies signed after February 1997 are assured shorthold agreements unless otherwise stated.

Assured tenancies are governed by the 1988 Housing Act, as amended by the 1996 Housing Act. It is to these Acts, or outlines of the Acts that the tenant must refer when intending to sign a tenancy for a residential property. For a tenancy to be assured, three conditions must be fulfilled:

1. The premises must be a dwelling house. This basically means any premises which can be lived in. Business premises will normally fall outside this interpretation.
2. There must exist a particular relationship between landlord and tenant. In other words there must exist a tenancy agreement. For example, a license to occupy, as in the case of students, or accommodation occupied as a result of work, cannot be seen as a tenancy. Following on from this, the accommodation must be let as a single unit. The tenant, who must be an individual, must normally be able to sleep, cook and eat in the accommodation. Sharing of bathroom facilities will not prevent a tenancy being an assured tenancy but shared cooking or other facilities, such as a living room, will.
3. The third requirement for an assured tenancy is that the tenant must occupy the dwelling as his or her only or principal home. In situations involving joint tenants at least one of them must occupy.

Tenancies that are not assured

A tenancy agreement will not be assured if one of the following conditions applies:

- The tenancy or the contract was entered into before 15th January 1989;

- If no rent is payable or if only a low rent amounting to less than two thirds of the present ratable value of the property is payable;

- If the premises are let for business purposes or for mixed residential and business purposes;

- If part of the dwelling house is licensed for the sale of liquor for consumption on the premises. This does not include the publican who lets out a flat;

- If the dwelling house is let with more than two acres of agricultural land;

- If the dwelling house is part of an agricultural holding and is occupied in relation to carrying out work on the holding;

- If the premises are let by a specified institution to students, i.e., halls of residence;

- If the premises are let for the purpose of a holiday;

- Where there is a resident landlord, e.g., in the case where the landlord has let one of his rooms but continues to live in the house;

- If the landlord is the Crown (the monarchy) or a government department. Certain lettings by the Crown are capable of being assured, such as some lettings by the Crown Estate Commissioners;

- If the landlord is a local authority, a fully mutual housing association (this is where you have to be a shareholder to be a tenant) a newly created Housing Action Trust or any similar body listed in the 1988 Housing Act.

- If the letting is transitional such as a tenancy continuing in its original form until phased out, such as:

- A protected tenancy under the 1977 Rent Act;
- Secure tenancy granted before 1st January 1989, e.g., from a local authority or housing association. These tenancies are governed by the 1985 Housing Act).

The Assured Shorthold tenancy

The assured shorthold tenancy as we have seen, is the most common form of tenancy used in the private sector. The main principle of the assured shorthold tenancy is that it is issued for a period of six months minimum and can be brought to an end by the landlord serving two months notice on the tenant. At the end of the six-month period the tenant, if given two months prior notice, must leave. If the tenant refuses to leave then the landlord can use a special 'fast track' procedure to get him/her out.

Any property let on an assured tenancy can be let on an assured shorthold, providing the following three conditions are met:

- The tenancy must be for a fixed term of not less than six months.
- The agreement cannot contain powers which enable the landlord to end the tenancy before six months. This does not include the right of the landlord to enforce the grounds for possession, which will be approximately the same as those for the assured tenancy (see below).
- A notice requiring possession at the end of the term is served two months before that date.
- A notice must be served before any rent increase giving one months clear notice and providing details of the rent increase.

If the landlord wishes to get possession of his/her property, in this case before the expiry of the contractual term, the landlord has to gain a court order. A notice of seeking possession must be served, giving fourteen days notice and following similar grounds of possession as an assured tenancy. *The landlord cannot simply tell a tenant to leave before the end of the agreed term.*

If the tenancy runs on after the end of the fixed term then the landlord can regain possession by giving the required two months notice, as mentioned above.

At the end of the term for which the assured shorthold tenancy has been granted, the landlord has an automatic right to possession. An assured shorthold tenancy will become periodic (will run from week to week) when the initial term of six months has elapsed and the landlord has not brought the tenancy to an end. A periodic tenancy is brought to an end with two months notice.

Assured shorthold tenants, can be evicted only on certain grounds some discretionary, some mandatory (see below). In order for the landlord of an assured shorthold tenant to regain possession of the property, other than issuing a s21 notice, a notice of seeking possession (of property) must be served, giving fourteen days notice of expiry and stating the ground for possession. This notice is similar to a notice to quit, discussed in the previous chapter. Following the fourteen days a court order must be obtained. Although gaining a court order is not complicated, a solicitor will usually be used. Court costs can be awarded against the tenant.

Security of tenure: The ways in which a tenant can lose their home as an assured shorthold tenant

There are a number of circumstances called grounds (mandatory and discretionary) whereby a landlord can start a court action to evict a tenant. The following are the *mandatory* grounds (where the judge must give the landlord possession) and *discretionary* grounds (where the judge does not have to give the landlord possession) on which a court can order possession if the home is subject to an assured tenancy.

The mandatory grounds for possession of a property

There are eight mandatory grounds for possession, which, if proved, leave the court with no choice but to make an order for possession. It is very important that you understand these.

Ground One is used where the landlord has served a notice, no later than at the beginning of the tenancy, warning the tenant that this ground may be used against him/her.

This ground is used where the landlord wishes to recover the property as his or her principal (first and only) home or the spouse's (wife's or husbands) principal home. *The ground is not available to a person who bought the premises for gain (profit) whilst they were occupied.*

Ground Two is available where the property is subject to a mortgage and if the landlord does not pay the mortgage, could lose the home.

Grounds Three and Four relate to holiday lettings.

Ground Five is a special one, applicable to ministers of religion.

Ground Six relates to the demolition or reconstruction of the property.

Ground Seven applies if a tenant dies and in his will leaves the tenancy to someone else: but the landlord must start proceedings against the new tenant within a year of the death if he wants to evict the new tenant.

Ground Eight concerns rent arrears. This ground applies if, both at the date of the serving of the notice seeking possession and at the date of the hearing of the action, the rent is at least 8 weeks in arrears. This is the main ground used by landlords when rent is not being paid. The landlord should understand that in order to get a court order for possession of property for rent arrears then, because of the short-term nature of the Assured shorthold, time is of the essence. If the tenancy is into the third month, it may be easier to wait and serve a two-month notice of termination and get a court order against the occupants separately. One of the advantages of a court order is that you will have details of the tenant's employers and can get an attachment of earnings against the tenant.

The discretionary grounds for possession of a property, which is let on an assured tenancy

As we have seen, the discretionary grounds for possession are those in relation to which the court has some powers over whether or not the landlord can evict. In other words, the final decision is left to the judge. Often the judge will prefer to grant a suspended order first, unless the circumstances are dramatic.

Ground Nine applies when suitable alternative accommodation is available or will be when the possession order takes effect. As we have seen, if the landlord wishes to obtain possession of his or her property in order to use it for other purposes then suitable alternative accommodation has to be provided.

Ground Ten deals with rent arrears as does *ground eleven*. These grounds are distinct from the mandatory grounds, as there does not have to be a fixed arrear in terms of time scale, e.g., 8 weeks. The judge, therefore, has some choice as to whether or not to evict. In practice, this ground will not be relevant to managers of assured shorthold tenancies.

Ground Twelve concerns any broken obligation of the tenancy. As we have seen with the protected tenancy, there are a number of conditions of the tenancy agreement, such as the requirement not to racially or sexually harass a neighbor. Ground Twelve will be used if these conditions are broken.

Ground Thirteen deals with the deterioration of the dwelling as a result of a tenant's neglect. This is connected with the structure of the property and is the same as for a protected tenancy. It puts the responsibility on the tenant to look after the premises.

Ground Fourteen concerns nuisance, annoyance and illegal or immoral use. This is where a tenant or anyone connected with the tenant has caused a nuisance to neighbors.

Ground 14A this ground deals with domestic violence.

Ground 15 concerns the condition of the furniture and tenants neglect. As Ground thirteen puts some responsibility on the tenant to look after the structure of the building so Ground Fifteen makes the tenant responsible for the furniture and fittings.

Ground 16 covers former employees. The premises were let to a former tenant by a landlord seeking possession and the tenant has ceased to be in that employment.

Ground 17 is where a person or that persons agents makes a false or reckless statement and this has caused the landlord to grant the tenancy under false pretences.

The description of the grounds above is intended as a guide only. For a fuller description please refer to the 1988 Housing Act, section 7, Schedule two,) as amended by the 1996 Housing Act) which is available at reference libraries.

Ch. 5

Joint Tenancies

Joint tenancies

Tenancy agreements

You have a joint tenancy if you and the other tenants all signed a single tenancy agreement with a landlord when you moved in. If each of you signed a separate agreement with the landlord, you have separate tenancies.

Right to rent

As we discussed, you can only become a private tenant if you have the right to rent. Each joint tenant must have the right to rent. A private landlord or letting agent must carry out a right to rent check before you sign up to a private tenancy.

Paying the rent when you're a joint tenant

Joint tenants are each jointly and individually responsible for paying the rent.

If one tenant moves out without giving notice or doesn't pay their share of the rent, the other joint tenants are responsible for paying it for them. If none of you pay your rent, your landlord can ask any one of you to pay the outstanding rent.

Tenancy deposits

The landlord normally takes a single deposit for the whole of the tenancy. Even if you and the other joint tenants paid separate or different shares to the landlord or agent. If one joint tenant fails to pay their share of the rent or if they cause damage to the property, the landlord is entitled to deduct the shortfall or the costs of the damage from the whole deposit.

You and the other joint tenants decide how to divide up the remaining deposit when it is returned.

Tenancy deposits when a joint tenant moves out

If you are replacing another tenant who is moving out, they may ask you to pay the deposit to them instead. This could cause problems. If the tenant who is moving out has caused any damage to the property or left any unpaid bills, the landlord can deduct these costs from the deposit when you move out. Get advice if you are in this situation. It might be better to ask the landlord to give a new tenancy agreement to you and the other tenants who are staying on.

How you can end a fixed-term joint tenancy

If you have a fixed-term tenancy (for example for 12 months) you can only the tenancy before the fixed term ends if:

- you, the other tenants and your landlord all agree that the tenancy can end early (this is called a 'surrender')
- there is a 'break clause' in your tenancy agreement, which allows you to give notice and end your tenancy early

- You need the agreement of the other joint tenants to end your tenancy early.

How to end a joint tenancy that isn't a fixed-term

If you don't have fixed-term tenancy or it has ended and not been renewed, you or any other joint tenant can end the tenancy by giving a valid notice to quit to the landlord. You can do this with or without the agreement of the other joint tenants. The tenancy ends for all the joint tenants. When the notice to quit expires none of you has the right to continue living there.

Leaving a joint tenancy

If you want to leave a joint tenancy and the others want to stay it is usually best to discuss it with the other joint tenants before you take any action.

If they don't want to move out, they can try to negotiate a new agreement with the landlord. The remaining tenants may be able to find another person to become a joint tenant with them. They must get the landlord's agreement for this. Or the remaining tenants could all agree to stay on and pay the rent between them.

However if the joint tenancy has not been ended the landlord could still ask you to pay any arrears if the rent is not fully paid, even if you are no longer living there.

Eviction of joint tenants

Your landlord cannot evict one joint tenant without evicting all the others. Your landlord may be able to end the tenancy and offer a new one to the remaining tenants. Talk to your landlord as soon as possible if you are in this situation and you want to stay.

Relationship breakdown

Your landlord could grant you a new tenancy in your name only if the joint tenancy with your ex-partner has been properly ended. You may also have other rights. For example:

- it may be possible for court to transfer the tenancy into your name – even if the other joint tenant won't agree to it
- it may be possible to stop the other joint tenant from ending the tenancy by applying for an occupation order or an injunction
- if you have experienced domestic violence, it may be possible to take legal action such as an injunction

Problems with other joint tenants

If you have a problem with another joint tenant you probably have to sort this out yourself. Landlords are usually reluctant to get involved, although council or housing associations are more likely to get involved than private landlords.

**

Ch. 6

Rent and Other Charges

The payment of rent and other financial matters

If a tenancy is protected under the Rent Act 1977, as described earlier there is the right to apply to the Rent Officer for the setting of a fair rent for the property. However, as described earlier, the incidence of Rent Act Protected Tenancies has diminished to almost zero.

The assured tenant

The assured tenant has far fewer rights in relation to rent control than the protected tenant. The Housing Act 1988 allows a landlord to charge whatever he likes. There is no right to a fair or reasonable rent with an assured tenancy. If the tenancy is assured then there will usually be a formula in the tenancy which will provide guidance for rent increases. If not then the landlord can set what rent he or she likes within reason. If the amount is unreasonable then the tenant can refer the matter to the local Rent Assessment Committee. The rent can sometimes be negotiated at the outset of the tenancy. This rent has to be paid as long as the contractual term of the tenancy lasts. Once the contractual term has expired, the landlord is entitled to continue to charge the same rent.

On expiry of an assured shorthold the landlord is free to grant a new tenancy and set the rent to a level that is compatible with the market.

Details of the local Rent Assessment Committee can be obtained from the Rent Officer Service at your local authority.

Local housing allowance (LHA) (housing benefit) for people who rent a home from a private landlord.

Local housing allowance is housing benefit for private sector tenants. It's usually paid directly to you and you pay your landlord. Local housing allowance is housing benefit that helps pay the rent and some service charges (if applicable) if you rent from a private landlord. It's a benefit administered by your local council. LHA has many of the same rules as housing benefit, but there are some extra rules that limit the amount of help you can get for a private rented home. LHA is usually paid direct to you rather than to your landlord.

Claim LHA

You can claim local housing allowance if you are a private tenant who needs help with paying the rent. You may be entitled to this housing benefit if you are working or if you claim benefits. Local Housing Allowance (LHA) is used to work out Housing Benefit for tenants who rent privately. How much you get is usually based on:

- where you live
- your household size
- your income - including benefits, pensions and savings (over £6,000)
- your circumstances

Your LHA claim is routinely reassessed after 12 months. Your claim may be reassessed at any time if your circumstances change.

How LHA is calculated

The amount of LHA you can get depends on your income and savings and if any non-dependants live with you, for example adult children.

The amount of LHA you receive also depends on the maximum rent allowed for properties in your area and the number of rooms the council decides you need.

You can rent a home of any size or price, but your housing benefit claim is limited. You have to make up any rent shortfall.

Maximum LHA amounts

There are limits on the amount of LHA you can get. The maximum weekly LHA rate limits (2019-2020) you are eligible for will depend on where you live. Local limits are based on the cheapest 30% of properties in an area. You should check with your local authority. for the current rates

Rooms allowed when calculating LHA

You are assessed as needing a bedroom for the following people in your home:

- an adult couple
- another person aged 16 or over
- any two children of the same sex up to the age of 16
- any two children regardless of sex under the age of 10
  any other child

An extra bedroom can be allowed if you:

- have a foster child or children
- have a severely disabled child who needs their own room
- or your partner are disabled and a carer provides regular overnight care
- have a child who is away on duty with the armed forces and intends to return home
- You cannot be allowed more than four bedrooms for the purposes of calculating your LHA.

If you're aged under 35

You are usually only entitled to LHA at the reduced shared accommodation rate if you are a single person under age 35 without children or you live in shared accommodation.

How often is housing benefit paid?

Payment of housing benefit depends on how often you pay rent. Housing benefit is not paid in advance. Each payment covers a past period. Private landlords usually expect rent to be paid in advance, so you need to budget for this.

When LHA can be paid direct to landlords

Your council must make your LHA payments direct to your landlord if:

- you have rent arrears of eight weeks or more
- deductions are being made from your benefits for rent arrears
- In some cases, the council can choose to pay your LHA direct to your landlord. They could do this if you have failed to pay the rent in the past or you have problems paying your rent because of

- a medical condition. The council can pay LHA direct to your landlord if this will help you keep your tenancy.

If you have support needs, the council can pay LHA to your landlord to encourage them to keep you as a tenant. The council will consult you and people supporting you before deciding to pay LHA direct to your landlord. This may include your doctor, support worker, probation officer and others who know about your situation.

Council Tax Support

If you are in receipt of benefits you may get help with your council tax through Council tax Support. Your local authority will advise you on this.

**

Ch. 7

The Right to Quiet Enjoyment of a Home

Earlier, we saw that when a tenancy agreement is signed, the landlord is contracting to give quiet enjoyment of the tenants home. This means that they have the right to live peacefully in the home without harassment.

The landlord is obliged not to do anything that will disturb the right to the quiet enjoyment of the home. The most serious breach of this right would be for the landlord to wrongfully evict a tenant.

Eviction: what can be done against unlawful eviction

It is a criminal offence for a landlord unlawfully to evict a residential occupier (whether or not a tenant!). The occupier has protection under the Protection from Eviction Act 1977 section 1(2). If the tenant or occupier is unlawfully evicted his/her first course should be to seek an injunction compelling the landlord to readmit him/her to the premises. It is an unfortunate fact but many landlords will attempt to evict tenants forcefully. In doing so they break the law.

The Deregulation Act 2015 has introduced a new provision which deals with 'retaliatory evictions'. This is where the landlord has decided to issue a s21 notice on the tenant because they have complained about the landlords service (for example repairs to the property) or unreasonable behaviour. If it can be proven that the notice was a 'retaliatory notice' then this will be invalid.

However, the landlord may, on termination of the tenancy, recover possession without a court order if the agreement was entered into after 15th January 1989 and it falls into one of the following six situations:

- The occupier shares any accommodation with the landlord and the landlord occupies the premises as his or her only or principal home.
- The occupier shares any of the accommodation with a member of the landlords family, that person occupies the premises as their only or principal home, and the landlord occupies as his or her only or principal home premises in the same building.
- The tenancy or license was granted temporarily to an occupier who entered the premises as a trespasser.
- The tenancy or license gives the right to occupy for the purposes of a holiday.
- The tenancy or license is rent-free.
- The license relates to occupation of a hostel.

There is also a section in the 1977 Protection from Eviction Act which provides a defense for otherwise unlawful eviction and that is that the landlord may repossess if it is thought that the tenant no longer lives on the premises. It is important to note that, in order for such action to be seen as a crime under the 1977 Protection from Eviction Act, the intention of the landlord to evict must be proved. However, there is another offence, namely harassment, which also needs to be proved. Even if the landlord is not guilty of permanently depriving a tenant of their home he/she could be guilty of harassment. Such actions as cutting off services, deliberately allowing the premises to fall into a state of disrepair, or even forcing unwanted sexual attentions, all constitute harassment and a breach of the right to *quiet enjoyment.*

The 1977 Protection from Eviction Act also prohibits the use of violence to gain entry to premises. Even in situations where the landlord has the right to gain entry without a court order it is an offence to use violence.

What can be done against unlawful evictions?

There are two main remedies for unlawful eviction: damages and, as stated above, an injunction.

The injunction

An injunction is an order from the court requiring a person to do, or not to do something. In the case of eviction the court can grant an injunction requiring the landlord to allow a tenant back into occupation of the premises. In the case of harassment an order can be made preventing the landlord from harassing the tenant. Failure to comply with an injunction is contempt of court and can result in a fine or imprisonment.

Damages

In some cases the tenant can press for *financial compensation* following unlawful eviction. Financial compensation may have to be paid in cases where financial loss has occurred or in cases where personal hardship alone has occurred. The tenant can also press for *special damages,* which means that the tenant may recover the definable out-of-pocket expenses. These could be expenses arising as a result of having to stay in a hotel because of the eviction. Receipts must be kept in that case. There are also *general damages*, which can be awarded in compensation for stress, suffering and inconvenience.

A tenant may also seek *exemplary damages* where it can be proved that the landlord has disregarded the law deliberately with the intention of making a profit out of the displacement of the tenant.

**

Ch. 8

Repairs-Landlords/Tenants Obligations

Repairs and improvements generally: The landlord and tenants obligations

Repairs are essential works to keep the property in good order. Improvements and alterations to the property, e.g. the installation of a shower. (see summary of disrepair cases at the end of the chapter).

As we have seen, most tenancies are periodic, i.e. week-to-week or month-to-month. If a tenancy falls into this category, or is a fixed-term tenancy for less than seven years, and began after October 1961, then a landlord is legally responsible for most major repairs to the flat or house.

If a tenancy began after 15th January 1989 then, in addition to the above responsibility, the landlord is also responsible for repairs to common parts and service fittings.

The area of law dealing with the landlord and tenants repairing obligations is the 1985 Landlord and Tenant Act, section 11.

This section of the Act is known as a covenant and cannot be excluded by informal agreement between landlord and tenant. In other words the landlord is legally responsible whether he or she likes it or not. Parties to a tenancy, however, may make an application to a court mutually to vary or exclude this section.

Example of repairs a landlord is responsible for:

- Leaking roofs and guttering.
- Rotting windows.
- Rising damp.
- Damp walls.
- Faulty electrical wiring.
- Dangerous ceilings and staircases.
- Faulty gas and water pipes.
- Broken water heaters and boilers.
- Broken lavatories, sinks or baths.

In shared housing the landlord must see that shared halls, stairways, kitchens and bathrooms are maintained and kept clean and lit.

Normally, tenants are responsible only for minor repairs, e.g., broken door handles, cupboard doors, etc. Tenants will also be responsible for decorations unless they have been damaged as a result of the landlord's failure to do repair.

A landlord will be responsible for repairs only if the repair has been reported. It is therefore important to report repairs in writing and keep a copy. If the repair is not carried out then action can be taken. Damages can also be claimed.

Compensation can be claimed, with the appropriate amount being the reduction in the value of the premises to the tenant caused by the landlord's failure to repair. If the tenant carries out the repairs then the amount expended will represent the decrease in value.

The tenant does not have the right to withhold rent because of a breach of repairing covenant by the landlord. However, depending on the repair, the landlord will not have a very strong case in court if rent is withheld.

Reporting repairs to landlords

The tenant has to tell the landlord or the person collecting the rent straight away when a repair needs doing. It is advisable that it is in writing, listing the repairs that need to be done. Once a tenant has reported a repair the landlord must do it within a reasonable period of time. What is reasonable will depend on the nature of the repair.

The tenants rights whilst repairs are being carried out

The landlord must ensure that the repairs are done in an orderly and efficient way with minimum inconvenience to the tenant If the works are disruptive or if property or decorations are damaged the tenant can apply to the court for compensation or, if necessary, for an order to make the landlord behave reasonably.

If the landlord genuinely needs the house empty to do the work he/she can ask the tenant to vacate it and can if necessary get a court order against the tenant.

A written agreement should be drawn up making it clear that the tenant can move back in when the repairs are completed and stating what the arrangements for fuel charges and rent are.

Can the landlord put the rent up after doing repairs?

If there is a service charge for maintenance, the landlord may be able to pass on the cost of the work(s).

Tenants rights to make improvements to a property

Unlike carrying out repairs the tenant will not normally have the right to insist that the landlord make actual alterations to the home. However, a tenant needs the following amenities and the law states that you should have:

- Bath or shower.
- Wash hand basin.
- Hot and cold water at each bath, basin or shower.
- An indoor toilet.

If these amenities do not exist then the tenant can contact the council's Environmental Health Officer. An improvement notice can be served on the landlord ordering him to put the amenity in.

Disabled tenants

As discussed previously, If a tenant is disabled he/she may need special items of equipment in the accommodation. The local authority may help in providing and, occasionally, paying for these.

The tenant will need to obtain the permission of the landlord. If you require more information then contact the social services department locally.

Houses in multiple occupation (HMO)

A landlord has extra legal responsibilities if the house or flat shared with other tenants is a house in multiple occupation (HMO). The extra rules are there to reduce the risk of fire and to make sure that people living in shared houses or flats have adequate facilities. From 1st October 2018, all landlords who fall within the HMO category must be licensed by the local authority for the area. A home is an HMO if:

- 3 or more unrelated people live there as at least 2 separate households – for example, 3 single people with their own rooms, or 2 couples each sharing a room the 3 or more people living there share basic amenities, such as a kitchen or bathroom. The requirement for the property to cover three or more stories of a property has now been removed and it is estimated that this change will mean that some 177,000 rental properties will now be classed as HMOs.

A home is a large HMO if both of the following apply:

- at least 5 tenants live there, forming more than 1 household
- They share toilet, bathroom or kitchen facilities with other tenants
- A household is either a single person or members of the same family who live together. A family includes people who are:
- married or living together - including people in same-sex relationships
- relatives or half-relatives, for example grandparents, aunts, uncles, siblings
- step-parents and step-children

An HMO could be a:

- house split into separate bedsits
- shared house or flat, where the sharers are not members of the same family
- hostel
- bed-and-breakfast hotel that is not just for holidays
- shared accommodation for students – although many halls of residence and other types of student accommodation owned by educational establishments are not classed as HMOs

Extra responsibilities of HMO landlords

Landlords of HMOs must make sure that:

- proper fire safety measures are in place, including working smoke alarms
- annual gas safety checks are carried out
- electrics are checked every 5 years
- the property is not overcrowded
- there are enough cooking and bathroom facilities for the number living there
- communal areas and shared facilities are clean and in good repair
- there are enough rubbish bins/bags

Responsibility for repairs in HMOs

A landlord is responsible for any repairs to communal areas of A home.

They are also responsible for repairs to:

- the structure and exterior of the house – including the walls, window frames and gutters

- water and gas pipes
- electrical wiring
- basins, sinks, baths and toilets
- fixed heaters (radiators) and water heaters

HMOs don't need to be licensed if they are managed or owned by a housing association or co-operative, a council, a health service or a police or fire authority.

Licences usually last for 5 years but some councils grant them for shorter periods. When deciding whether to issue or renew a licence, the council checks that:

- the property meets an acceptable standard. For example, it looks at whether the property is large enough for the occupants and if it is well managed
- the landlord is a 'fit and proper' person
- Minimum bedroom size for HMOs

If a landlord applied for a HMO licence on or after 1 October 2018 or has renewed it since, bedroom sizes must be at least:

6.51 square metres for an adult

10.22 square metres for two adults

4.64 square metres for a child under 10 years old

Some councils may set higher standards for bedroom sizes.

If a room is used as bedroom and doesn't meet the size requirement, the council may allow a landlord up to 18 months to make the room larger or move you to a different bedroom. The council can prosecute or fine a landlord if a bedroom is smaller than standards allow.

Landlord penalties for not having an HMO licence

A landlord can be fined and ordered to repay up to 12 months' rent if tenants live in a HMO that should be licensed but isn't. A tenants can apply for a rent repayment order within a year of the HMO being unlicensed, and also any housing benefit or universal credit tenants have used to help them pay rent will be reclaimed by the council.

Many people living in HMOs have an assured shorthold tenancy. If a tenant has an assured shorthold tenant and the HMO should be licensed but isn't, a landlord won't be able to evict tenants using a section 21 notice.

The council can prosecute landlords of HMOs, or any manager they have employed, if they break the law. In extreme cases, the council can take over the management of the property.

Safety generally for all landlords-the regulations

The main product safety regulations relevant to the lettings industry are:

Gas safety

The Gas safety (Installation and use) Regulations 1998

The Gas Cooking Appliances (safety) Regulations 1989

Heating Appliances(Fireguard) (safety) Regulations 1991

Gas Appliances(Safety) Regulations 1995

All of the above are based on the fact that the supply of gas and the appliances in a dwelling are safe. A Gas Safety certificate is required to validate this.

Furniture Safety

Furniture and Furnishings (Fire) (Safety) Regulations 1988 and 1993 (as amended). Landlords and lettings agents are included in these regulations. The regulations set high standards for fire resistance for domestic upholstered furniture and other products containing upholstery.

The Regulations apply to any upholstered furniture manufactured after 1st January 1950 intended for use in a dwelling including:

- All types of upholstered seating including chairs, settees, padded stools and ottomans. Children's furniture, foot stools, sofa-beds, futons and other convertibles, bean bags and floor cushions nursery furniture and upholstered items designed to contain a baby or small child. Domestic upholstered furniture that is supplied in kit form for self-assembly. Second hand furniture Upholstered head-boards, footboards and side rails of beds.

- Furniture for use in the open air (garden and outdoor furniture) which is suitable for use in a dwelling (homes or caravans) such as conservatory furniture

- Upholstery in caravans (although not vehicles or boats) and Cane furniture which includes upholstery.

- Divans, bed-bases, mattresses, pillows, and mattress pads (toppers) scatter cushions and seat pads (FILLING MATERIAL ONLY)

- Permanent covers for furniture (textiles, coated textiles, leather etc) Loose and stretch covers for furniture. Covers for non-visible parts of furniture

- Foam and non-foam filling material for furniture

What items are not covered?

- Upholstered furniture manufactured before 1st January 1950

- Materials used solely to recover pre -1950 furniture

- Sleeping Bags

- Bed Clothes or Duvets

- Loose Mattress Covers

- Pillow Cases

- Curtains

- Carpets

Upholstered articles (i.e. beds, sofas, armchairs etc) must have fire resistant filling material.

Upholstered articles must have passed a match resistant test or, if of certain kinds (such as cotton or silk) be used with a fire resistant interliner.

The combination of the cover fabric and the filling material must have passed a cigarette resistance test.

The landlord should inspect property for non-compliant items before letting and replace with compliant items.

Electrical Safety

Electrical Equipment (Safety) Regulations 1994

Plugs and Sockets etc. (Safety) Regulations 1994.

Electrical hazards are also covered by the Housing Health and safety Rating System under the Housing Act 2004. In the case of commercial property and houses in multiple occupation there is a statutory duty under the Regulatory Reform Fire Safety Order 2005 for the responsible person (the property manager) to carry out annual Fire Safety Risk Assessments, which include electrical safety risks.

The Electrical Equipment Regulations came into force in January 1995. Both sets of regulations relate to the supply of electrical equipment designed with a working voltage of between 50 and 1000 volts ac. (or between 75 and 1000 volts dc.) the regulations cover all the mains voltage household electrical goods including cookers, kettles, toasters, electric blankets, washing machines, immersion heaters etc. The regulations do not apply to items attached to land. This is generally considered to exclude the fixed

85

wiring and built in appliances (e.g. central heating systems) from the regulations. Lettings agents and landlords should take the following action:

Essential:

Check all electrical appliances in all managed properties on a regular fixed term basis. Remove unsafe items and keep a record of checks.

Recommended:

- Have appliances checked by a qualified electrical engineer
- Avoid purchasing second hand electrical items
- There is no specific requirement for regular testing under the regulations. However, it is recommended that a schedule of checks, say on an annual basis, is put in place.

For more information on electrical safety visit www.landlordzone.co.uk/information/electrical-safety.
This is a particularly good site.

Tougher rules announced for electrical inspections for rented homes in the UK (January 2019)

Rules on electrical safety in the UK's private rented sector are being tightened to ensure mandatory electrical checks are carried out by competent and qualified inspectors. The tougher rules will mean greater protection for tenants and help drive up standards in the lettings sector.

Landlords will be legally required to ensure that the inspectors they hire to carry out safety inspections have the necessary competence and qualifications to do so with tough financial penalties for those who fail to comply. Ministers will also publish new guidance which sets out the minimum level of competence and qualifications necessary for those carrying out these important inspections, meaning both landlords and tenants can be assured their home is safe from electrical faults.

The availability of grants

There are a number of grants available to landlords at any one time which will enable improvements to take place to a property. One of the main grants is the Disabled facilities Grant. However, there are more and your local authority can tell you what is available.

Rgulations on Smoke and Carbon Monoxide detectors

From October 2015, all landlords, regardless of whether public or private sector, arequired to install working smoke and carbon monoxide alarms in their properties, on each floor. The carbon monoxide alarms need to be placed in high risk areas, i.e., where there are gas appliances such as boilers or fires. Carbon monoxide detectors will not be required in properties where there are no gas or solid fuel appliances. A civil penalty of up to £5,000 will apply to landlords who fail to comply with this legislation.

Obligations on Landlords to upgrade and maintain insulation

From April 2018, properties rented out in the private rented sector is required to have a minimum energy performance rating of E. The regulations apply to new lets and renewals of tenancies, and will apply to all existing tenancies on 1st April 2020. It will be against the law to rent a property which has a rating lower than E, unless there is an applicable exemption.

Legionnaire's disease

It is the responsibility of all landlords to undertake a risk assessment to prevent the spread of the Legionella bacteria, which can be found in a property's water systems and can lead to Legionnaires' disease if inhaled.

Legionnaires' disease is a pneumonia-like illness caused by Legionella bacteria and can be fatal. It is one of several conditions included within the Legionellosis group.

Although the risks are generally very low in residential property, health and safety legislation in the UK requires landlords to carry out risk assessments to control the exposure to tenants of Legionella.

The risk of Legionnaires' disease is likely to be higher in properties that are left empty and where water may be left to stand in both hot and cold systems, thus increasing the opportunity for the bacteria to multiply in the standing water.

As such, it is vital landlords ensure water systems are used at least once a week. And if a property is set to remain empty for several months, it may be worth draining the system to prevent the possibility of bacteria developing to unacceptable levels.

To minimise or eliminate the risk posed by Legionella, landlords should:

• Maintain cold water below 20 degrees C, as Legionella thrives in water between 20 and 45 degrees C

• Ensure showers and taps that are used infrequently - such as those in spare bedrooms - are periodically flushed through with running water

• Cover water tanks so mice, birds, insects and other creatures cannot gain access

• Remove unnecessary pipes, such as those leading to appliances that are no longer used

Signs of Legionella include:

• Cold water running warm

• Water that is discoloured or contains debris

• A malfunctioning boiler or hot water system

Sanitation health and hygiene generally

Local authorities have a duty to serve an owner with a notice requiring the provision of a WC when a property has insufficient sanitation, sanitation meaning toilet waste disposal.

They will also serve notice if it is thought that the existing sanitation is inadequate and is harmful to health or is a nuisance.

Local authorities have similar powers under various Public Health Acts to require owners to put right bad drains and sewers, also food storage facilities and vermin, plus the containing of disease.

The Environmental Health Department, if it considers the problem bad enough will serve a notice requiring the landlord to put the defect right. In certain cases the local authority can actually do the work and require the landlord to pay for it. This is called work in default.

**

Ch. 9

___

What Should Be Provided Under the Tenancy

___

Furniture

A landlords decision whether or not to furnish property will depend on the sort of tenant that he is aiming to find. The actual legal distinction between a furnished property and an unfurnished property has faded into insignificance.

If a landlord does let a property as furnished then the following would be the absolute minimum:

- Seating, such as sofa and armchair

- Cabinet or sideboard

- Kitchen tables and chairs

- Cooker and refrigerator

- Bedroom furniture

Even unfurnished lets, however, are expected to come complete with a basic standard of furniture, particularly carpets and kitchen goods. If the landlord does supply electrical equipment then he or she is able to disclaim any repairing responsibility for it, but this must be mentioned in the tenancy agreement.

Insurance

Strictly speaking, there is no duty on either landlord or tenant to insure the property. However, it is highly advisable for the landlord to provide buildings insurance as he/she stands to lose a lot more in the event of fire or other disaster than the tenant. A landlord letting property for a first time would be well advised to consult his/ her insurance company before letting as there are different criteria to observe when a property is let and not to inform the company could invalidate the policy.

At the end of the tenancy

The tenancy agreement will normally spell out the obligations of the tenant at the end of the term. Essentially, the tenant will have an obligation to:

- have kept the interior clean and tidy and in a good state of repair and decoration
- have not caused any damage
- have replaced anything that they have broken
- replace or pay for the repair of anything that they have damaged
- pay for the laundering of the linen
- pay for any other laundering
- put anything that they have moved or removed back to how it was. Sometimes a tenancy agreement will include for the tenants paying for anything that is soiled at their own expense, although sensible wear and tear is allowed for.

The landlord will normally be able to recover any loss from the deposit that the tenant has given on entering the premises. However, sometimes, the tenants will withhold rent for the last month in order to recoup their deposit. This has become more difficult since the introduction of the tenancy deposit schemes, described earlier. It is up to the landlord to negotiate re-imbursement for any damage caused, but this should be within reason. There is a remedy, which can be pursued in the Small Claims court if the tenants refuse to pay but this is rarely successful.

A word on inventories

The Tenancy Deposit Scheme, has released new guidance on inventory reports to support landlords and letting agents ahead of the introduction of the Tenant Fees Act in June 2019.

Also known as the Tenant Fee Ban, the new law – which will apply to letting agents in England – means tenants cannot be charged for a number of extra services, including the provision of inventories. Landlords might then have to cover this cost themselves, rather than the charging or splitting costs with tenants. Without this option, some letting agents may choose to take the service in-house to minimise costs.

**

Ch. 10

Regaining Possession of a Property

As we have mentioned, currently there is a consultation in progress concerning scrapping s21 notices, in order to attempt to try to regain more security in the private lettings market. Until then, the current s21 rules are outlined below.

Fast-track possession

A landlord cannot serve a s21 notice (Form 6A) on an assured shorthold tenant until after the first four months of a tenancy (if it is for a six month period). This brings the tenancy to an end on the day of expiry, i.e. on the day of expiry of the six month period,

Rules for Section 21 notices

If the tenancy started or was renewed on or after 1 October 2015 a landlord will need to use the new prescribed Section 21 notice Form (6a). Form 6A has replaced both S21 and S8 Notices although the Form still relates to S21 and S6 of the Housing Act.

Section 21 (Form 6A) pre-requisites

A landlord cannot serve a valid Form 6A notice if:

- They have taken a deposit and not protected and/or served the prescribed information and/or

- They have failed to obtained a license for an HMO property which requires one

If the tenancy was in England and started or was renewed on or after 1 October 2015 a landlord must also have served on their tenant (and you should get proof of service for all these:

- an EPC

- a Gas Safety Certificate, and

- the latest version of the Government's "How to Rent" Guide.

- Which deposit scheme the tenants deposit is in

Plus a landlord cannot serve a section 21 notice if their Local Authority has served one of 3 specified notices (the most important being an improvement notice) on them within the past six months in respect of the poor condition of the rental property.

Also, if the tenant complained about the issues covered by the notice prior to this – any Section 21 notice served since the complaint and before the Local Authority notice was served will also be invalid.

The notice period must not be less than two months and must not end before the end of the fixed term (if this has not ended at the time the landlord served their notice)

If this is a periodic tenancy where the period (rent payment period) is more than monthly (e.g., a quarterly or six month periodic tenancy), then the notice period must be at least one full tenancy period.

The notice period does not have to end on a particular day in the month, as was required under the old rules – the landlord just needs to make sure that the notice period is sufficient – minimum of 2 months.

On expiry of the notice, if it is the landlord's intention to take possession of the property then the tenants should leave. It is worthwhile writing a letter to the tenants one month before expiry reminding them that they should leave.

In the event of the tenant refusing to leave, then the landlord has to then follow a process termed 'fast track possession'. This entails filling in the appropriate forms (N5B) which can be downloaded from Her Majesty's Court Service Website www.justice.gov.uk.

Assuming that a valid Form 6A notice has been served on the tenant, the accelerated possession proceedings can begin and the forms completed and lodged with the court dealing with the area where the property is situated. In order to grant the accelerated possession order the court will require the following:

- The assured shorthold agreement
- The section 21 notice (Form 6A)
- Evidence of service of the notice

The best form of service of the Form 6A notice is by hand. If a landlord has already served the notice then evidence that the tenant has received it will be required. Having the correct original paperwork is of the utmost importance. Without this, the application will fail and delays will be incurred.

If the tenant disputes the possession proceedings in any way they will have 14 days to reply to the court. If the case is well founded and the paperwork is in order then there should be no case for defence. Once the accelerated possession order has been granted then this will need to be served on the tenant, giving them 14 days to vacate. In certain circumstances, if the tenant pleads hardship the court can grant extra time to leave, six weeks as opposed to two weeks. If they still do not vacate then an application will need to be made to court for a bailiffs warrant to evict the tenants.

Accelerated possession proceedings cannot be used against the tenant for rent arrears. It will be necessary to follow the procedure below.

An accelerated possession order remains in force for six years from the date it was granted.

Going to court to end the tenancy

There may come a time when a landlord needs to go to court to regain possession of their property. This will usually arise when the contract has been breached by the tenant, for non-payment of rent or for some other breach such as nuisance or harassment. As we have seen, a tenancy can be brought to an end in a court on one of the grounds for possession. However, as the tenancy will usually be an assured shorthold then it is necessary for the landlord to consider whether they are in a position to give two months notice and withhold the deposit, as opposed to going to court. The act of withholding the deposit will entail the landlord refusing to authorize the payment to the tenant online. This then brings arbitration into the frame. Deposit schemes have an arbitration system as an integral part of the scheme.

If a landlord decides, for whatever reason, to go to court, then any move to regain a property for breach of agreement will commence in the county court in the area in which the property is. The first steps in ending the tenancy will necessitate the serving of a notice of seeking possession Form 6A using one of the Grounds for Possession detailed earlier in the book. If the tenancy is protected then 28 days must be given, the notice must be in prescribed form and served on the tenant personally (preferably).

If the tenancy is an assured shorthold, which is more often the case now, then 14 days notice of seeking possession can be used. In all cases the ground to be relied upon must be clearly outlined in the notice. If the case is more complex, then this will entail a particulars of claim being prepared, usually by a solicitor, as opposed to a standard possession form.

A fee is paid when sending the particulars to court, which should be checked with the local county court. The standard form which the landlord uses for routine rent arrears cases is called the N119 and the accompanying summons is called the N5. Both of these forms can be obtained from the court or from www.courtservice.gov. When completed, the forms are sent in duplicate to the county court and a copy retained for for the landlord.

The court will send a copy of the particulars of claim and the summons to the tenant. They will send the landlord a form which gives them a case number and court date to appear, known as the return date. On the return date, the landlord should arrive at court at least 15 minutes early.

Complainants can represent themselves in simple cases but are advised to use a solicitor for more contentious cases.

If the tenant is present then they will have a chance to defend themselves.

A number of orders are available. However, if you a person has gone to court on the mandatory ground eight then if the fact is proved then they will get possession immediately. If not, then the judge can grant an order, suspended whilst the tenant finds time to pay.

In a lot of cases, it is more expedient for a landlord to serve notice-requiring possession, if the tenancy has reached the end of the period, and then wait two months before the property is regained. This saves the cost and time of going to court particularly if the ground is one of nuisance or other, which will involve solicitors.

In many cases, if landlords are contemplating going to court and have never been before and do not know the procedure then it is best to use a solicitor to guide the case through.

Costs can be recovered from the tenant, although this will depend on their means. If possession is regained midway through the contractual term then the landlord will have to complete the possession process by use of bailiff, pay a fee and fill in another form, Warrant for Possession of Land.

If a landlord has reached the end of the contractual term and wish to recover their property then a fast track procedure is available which entails gaining an order for possession and bailiff's order by post. This can be used in cases with the exception of rent arrears.

**

Ch. 11

Public Sector Tenancies

Although this book is about the rights of the private tenant, there may come a time when it has been possible to gain access to the public sector. In that case, a knowledge of the public sector and rights and obligations will be necessary.

Renting from a social housing landlord

You are a tenant of a social housing landlord if you are a tenant of a local authority. These are district councils and London borough councils; or a housing association; or a housing co-operative.

Local authority tenants

If you are a tenant of a local authority you are likely to be a secure tenant or an introductory tenant. In England, from 1 April 2012, local authorities can also grant flexible tenancies.

Housing association and housing co-operative tenants
Tenancy began before 15 January 1989

If you are a housing association or housing co-operative tenant and your tenancy began before 15 January 1989, you will be a secure tenant. For details about the rights a secure tenant has, see below.

Tenancy began on or after 15 January 1989

If you are a housing association or housing co-operative tenant and your tenancy began on or after 15 January 1989, you are likely to be an assured tenant. Some association tenants may be starter tenants for the first 12 to 18 months. A starter tenancy is a type of assured shorthold tenancy. In England, from 1 April 2012, housing associations can use assured shorthold tenancies for tenancies other than starter tenancies.

Rights of secure tenants

As a secure tenant you have the right to stay in the accommodation unless your landlord can convince the court that there are special reasons to evict you, for example, you have rent arrears, damaged property or broken some other term of the agreement. As well as the right to stay in your home as long as you keep to the terms of the tenancy, you will also have other rights by law.

These include the right:

- to have certain repairs carried out by your landlord
- to carry out certain repairs and to do improvements yourself - see under heading Repairs and improvements
- to sublet part of your home with your landlord's permission
- to take in lodgers without your landlord's permission
- to exchange your home with certain other social housing tenants
- if you are a local authority tenant, the right to vote to transfer to another landlord
- to be kept informed about things relating to your tenancy

- to buy your home.

- if you are a housing association tenant whose tenancy started before 15 January 1989, the right to a 'fair rent' - see under heading Fixing and increasing the rent

- for your spouse, civil partner, other partner or in some cases a resident member of your family, to take over the tenancy on your death (the right of 'succession')

- to assign (pass on) the tenancy to a person who has the right of 'succession' to the tenancy. This is sometimes difficult to enforce

- if you are a local authority tenant, to take over the management of the estate with other tenants by setting up a Tenant Management Organisation

- not to be discriminated against because of your disability, gender reassignment, pregnancy and maternity, race, religion or belief, sex or sexual orientation.

You will usually have a written tenancy agreement which may give you more rights than those set out above.

Complaints about secure tenancies

Each social housing landlord must have a clear policy and procedure on dealing with complaints. You should have the opportunity to complain in a range of ways. If after using your landlord's complaints procedure you are still dissatisfied, you can complain to an Ombudsman about certain problems. In England, if you are a local authority tenant this will be the Local Government Ombudsman, and if you are a housing association tenant it will be the Housing Ombudsman. If you have suffered discrimination, you can complain about this to the Ombudsman. In Wales, you can complain to the Public Services Ombudsman for Wales.

Rights of assured tenants

As an assured tenant you have the right to stay in your accommodation unless your landlord can convince the court there are reasons to evict you, for example, that there are rent arrears, damage to the property, or that another of the terms of the agreement has been broken.

As an assured tenant you can enforce your rights, for example, to get repairs done, without worrying about getting evicted. As well as the right to stay in your home as long as you keep to the terms of the tenancy you will also have other rights by law including:-

* the right to have the accommodation kept in a reasonable state of repair
* the right to carry out minor repairs yourself and to receive payment for these from your landlord - see under heading Repairs and improvements
* the right for your spouse, civil partner or other partner to take over the tenancy on your death (the right of 'succession')
* the right not to be treated unfairly by your landlord because of your disability, gender reassignment, pregnancy and maternity, race, religion or belief, sex or sexuality.

You will usually have a written tenancy agreement which may give you more rights than those set out above.

Complaints about assured tenancies

Each housing association must have a clear policy and procedure on dealing with complaints. You should have the opportunity to complain in a range of ways. If after using your landlord's complaints procedure you are still dissatisfied, you can complain in England, to the Housing Ombudsman, or in Wales, to the Public Services Ombudsman for Wales.

Starter tenancies and assured shorthold tenancies

A starter tenancy is the name often used by housing associations to describe an assured shorthold tenancy. Starter tenancies are probationary tenancies which allow a landlord to evict you more easily if you break the terms of your tenancy agreement.

A starter tenancy generally lasts for 12 months, although they can be extended to 18 months. As long as no action has been taken by the landlord to end the tenancy within the starter period, the starter tenant can then become an assured or longer-term assured shorthold tenant in England, or an assured tenant in Wales.

In England, housing associations can use assured shorthold tenancies for tenancies other than starter tenancies. They are likely to last for a fixed term of five years or more, but in some cases will last for two years. These tenancies may also be on 'affordable rent' terms.

In England, if you have an assured shorthold tenancy of a fixed term of two years or more with a housing association landlord, you will generally have similar rights to an assured tenant. However, if you have a fixed term tenancy, you only have the right to stay in your home for the length of the fixed term.

Complaints about starter and assured shorthold tenancies

Each housing association must have a clear policy and procedure on dealing with complaints. You should have the opportunity to complain in a range of ways. If after using your landlord's complaints procedure you are still dissatisfied, you can complain in England, to the Housing Ombudsman, or in Wales, to the Public Services Ombudsman for Wales.

Fixing and increasing the rent-Secure tenants
Local authority tenancies

Rents for local authority tenants are fixed according to the local authority's housing policy and the amount of money they get from central government. You cannot control the amount of rent payable, but may be able to claim housing benefit to help pay it.

Housing association and housing co-operative tenancies which began before 15 January 1989

If you are a housing association or housing co-operative tenant whose tenancy started before 15 January 1989 you are a secure tenant, but your rent is generally a 'fair rent' registered by the Rent Officer. The housing association or co-operative will usually have had the rent registered.

Once a rent has been registered, a new rent cannot usually be considered for the accommodation for two years. The rent can only be increased if:-

- you ask for a new fair rent assessment after two years
- your landlord asks for a new fair rent assessment after one year and nine months, although any new rent would not become effective until the end of two years.

An application for a rent increase can be made earlier, but only if the tenancy has changed drastically or if you and your landlord apply together. If you need help paying the rent you may be able to claim housing benefit.

Assured tenants-Housing association or housing co-operative tenancies which began on or after 15 January 1989

Many housing association tenants whose tenancy started on or after 15 January 1989 are assured tenants. If you are an assured tenant, your rent is the rent you agreed to pay your landlord at the beginning of the tenancy and should be covered in your tenancy agreement. The tenancy agreement should also state when and how the rent can be increased.

In England, most housing associations and housing co-operatives are registered with the Homes and Communities Agency and must follow standards and procedures set down by this regulatory body. They are sometimes known as social landlords. They set rents in accordance with government guidance and tenants have to be given clear information about how their rent and service charges are set and how they can be changed.

You may have the right to apply to a Rent Assessment Committee if you do not agree to a rent increase.

In Wales, housing associations must manage their housing to standards set by the Welsh Government. You must be informed in writing, and in advance about any changes in your rent. You should be given at least 28 days notice of any increase. You may have the right to apply to a Rent Assessment Committee if you do not agree to a rent increase.

If you are a housing association tenant in Wales, there is a leaflet explaining your rights called The Guarantee for Housing Association Residents. You can find this on the Welsh Government website at: www.new.wales.gov.uk.

If you want to apply to a Rent Assessment Committee you should consult an experienced adviser, for example, a Citizens Advice Bureau. If you need help paying the rent you may be able to claim housing benefit. You may also be entitled to other benefits if you are on a low income or you are unemployed.

To work out which other benefits you may be entitled to, you should consult an experienced adviser, for example, a Citizens Advice Bureau.

Affordable rent

Affordable rent is a type of social housing provided in England by social housing landlords.

The rent is called 'affordable' but it is a higher rent than would normally be charged for social housing. The landlord can charge up to 80% of what it would cost if you were renting the property privately. The extra money from affordable rent homes goes towards building more new social housing.

In most cases, tenancies on affordable rent terms are granted by housing associations. Where the landlord is a housing association, the type of tenancy granted is either an assured or an assured shorthold tenancy. In some cases, a local authority may grant a tenancy on affordable rent terms. Where it does, the tenancy type is either a secure or a flexible tenancy.

An affordable rent can be increased once a year. The maximum amount that an affordable rent can be increased by is Retail Price Index (RPI) + 0.5 %. If you are on benefits or have a low income you may qualify for housing benefit to help pay some or all of the affordable rent.

Repairs and improvements

As a tenant you have the right to have your accommodation kept in a reasonable state of repair. You have also an obligation to look after the accommodation. The tenancy agreement may give more details of both your landlord's and your responsibilities in carrying out repairs and you should check this. We have discussed repairs earlier in the book.

Certain repairs will almost always be your landlord's responsibility, whether or not they are specifically mentioned in the tenancy agreement. These are:-

- the structure and exterior of the premises (such as walls, floors and window frames), and the drains, gutters and external pipes. If the property is a house, the essential means of access to it, such as steps from the street, are also included in 'structure and exterior'. It also includes garden paths and steps
- the water and gas pipes and electrical wiring (including, for example, taps and sockets)
- the basins, sinks, baths and toilets
- fixed heaters (for example, gas fires) and water heaters but not gas or electric cookers.

The Right to repair

Tenants of local authorities and other social landlords (including housing associations) can use 'right to repair' schemes to claim compensation for repairs which the landlord does not carry out within a set timescale.

Under the scheme, if repairs are not carried out within a fixed time scale, you can notify your landlord that you want a different contractor to do the job. The local authority must appoint a new contractor and set another time limit. You can then claim compensation if the repair is not carried out within the new time limit.

As a local authority tenant, you can currently use the 'right to repair' scheme for repairs which your landlord estimates would cost up to £250. You can also claim up to £50 compensation. Twenty types of repairs qualify for the scheme, including insecure doors, broken entry phone systems, blocked sinks and leaking roofs.

A repair will not qualify for the scheme if the local authority has fewer than 100 properties, is not responsible for the repair or if the authority decides it would cost more than £250.

If you're the tenant of another social landlord, such as a housing association, you are entitled to compensation if you report a repair or maintenance problem which affects your health, safety or security and your landlord fails twice to make the repair within the set timescale.

There is a flat rate award which is currently £10, plus £2 a day up to a total of £50, for each day the repair remains outstanding. A maximum cost for an eligible repair may be set by the individual landlord.

Improvements

As a local authority tenant if you make certain improvements to your home, for example, loft insulation, draught proofing, new baths, basins and toilets and security measures, you can apply for compensation for doing so when you move out. You will not be eligible for this compensation if you buy your home.

Disabled tenants

If you are disabled, you may be able to have alterations carried out to your home. You may first have to get the need for any alterations assessed by the social services department. Alterations could include the installation of a stair lift or hoist or adaptation of a bathroom or toilet. If you want to get an alteration carried out you should consult an experienced adviser, for example, at a Citizens Advice Bureau.

A disabled tenant may also be able to get a disabled facilities grant to make the home more suitable.

Gas appliances

Your landlord must make sure that any gas appliances in residential premises are safe. They must arrange for safety checks on appliances and fittings to be carried out at least once every twelve months. The inspection must be carried out by someone who is registered with Gas Safety Register. Their website is: www.gassaferegister.co.uk. The landlord must also keep a record of the date of the check, any problems identified and any action taken. As the tenant, you have the right to see this record as long as you give reasonable notice. If your landlord does not arrange for checks or refuses to allow you to see the record of the check, you could contact the local Health and Safety Executive office.

The right to stay in the accommodation

This is an outline of the rights you have as a tenant of a local authority, housing association or housing co-operative to stay in your accommodation and how you can be evicted.

Secure tenants

As a secure tenant you have the right to stay in the accommodation as long as you keep to the terms of the tenancy agreement with your landlord. However, if the tenancy agreement is broken, for example, because of rent arrears or nuisance to neighbours, your landlord can serve a notice on you and apply to the county court for eviction.

A social housing landlord can only evict you if they give you the proper notice and if one of the 'grounds for possession' applies.

What constitutes 'grounds for possession' is complicated and someone whose landlord is seeking eviction should consult an experienced adviser, for example, at a Citizens Advice Bureau.

The landlord must apply to the county court to seek possession of the property and a secure tenant can only be evicted if the court grants a possession order to the landlord.

Assured tenants

As an assured tenant you have the right to stay in the accommodation as long as you keep to the terms of the tenancy agreement with your landlord. However, if the tenancy agreement is broken, for example, because of rent arrears or nuisance to neighbours, your landlord can serve a notice on you. The housing association will then have to obtain a possession order from the county court by proving that one of the 'grounds for possession' applies. We discussed grounds for possession earlier in the book.

Social housing tenancies and discrimination

When renting accommodation from a local authority, housing association or other social landlord, they must not discriminate against you because of your disability, gender reassignment, pregnancy and maternity, race, religion or belief, sex or sexual orientation. This means that they are not allowed to:

- rent a property to you on worse terms than other tenants
- treat you differently from other tenants in the way you are allowed to use facilities such as a laundry or a garden
- evict or harass you because of discrimination

111

- charge you higher rent than other tenants
- refuse to re-house you because of discrimination
- refuse to carry out repairs to your home because of disrimination
- refuse to make reasonable changes to a property or a term in the tenancy agreement which would allow a disabled person to live there.

If you think your landlord is discriminating against you, you should get advice from an experienced adviser, for example, at a Citizens Advice Bureau.

Introductory tenants -who is an introductory tenant?

Some local authorities make all new tenants introductory tenants for the first 12 months of the tenancy.

Rights of introductory tenants

Introductory tenants have some but not all of the rights of secure tenants. The following table shows your rights as an introductory tenant compared with secure tenants.

Statutory right	Secure tenant	Introductory tenant
Right to succession by partners or in some cases family members	yes	yes
Right to repair	yes	yes
Right to assign	yes	no
Right to buy	yes	no, but period spent as an introductory tenant counts

Statutory right	Secure tenant	Introductory tenant
Right to take in lodgers	yes	no
Right to sub-let part of your home	yes	no
Right to do improvements	yes	no
Right to exchange your home with certain other tenants	yes	no
Right to vote prior to transfer to new landlord	yes	no
Right to be consulted on housing management issues	yes	yes
Right to be consulted on decision to delegate housing management	yes	yes
Right to participate in housing management contract monitoring	yes	yes

Ending an introductory tenancy

At the end of the twelve months, provided there have been no possession proceedings against you, the introductory tenancy will usually be converted by your landlord to a secure tenancy. However, your landlord may decide to extend the introductory tenancy for a further six months. If this happens, you will be told the reasons for the decision and given the chance to ask for the decision to be reviewed.

Possession proceedings

It is very easy for a landlord to evict an introductory tenant. If you have received a notice from the landlord stating that they intend to evict you and

113

take possession of the property, you should immediately consult an experienced adviser, for example, at a Citizens Advice Bureau.

Flexible tenants

Flexible tenancies are a type of tenancy that can be granted by local authority landlords in England, from 1 April 2012. Not all local authorities offer them.

A flexible tenancy is similar to a local authority secure tenancy. However, a secure tenancy is periodic, which means that it lasts for an indefinite period of time. Periodic tenancies are often called 'lifetime tenancies'. In contrast, a flexible tenancy lasts for a fixed period of time. In most cases, a flexible tenancy will last for at least five years.

A local authority has to serve a written notice on you before a flexible tenancy can start. The notice must tell you that the tenancy you're being offered is a flexible tenancy, and what the terms of the tenancy are.

Flexible tenants have a number of legal rights, many of which are similar to the rights of secure tenants. For example, the right to pass on your tenancy when you're alive or when you die, the right to exchange your home with certain other tenants, and the right to buy your home.

A local authority doesn't have to grant you another tenancy when the fixed term of the flexible tenancy comes to an end. You can ask the local authority to review its decision not to grant you another tenancy. The review will consider if your landlord has followed its policies and procedures when making that decision.

If you are not given another tenancy when your flexible tenancy comes to an end, the local authority will take action to evict you.

**

Ch. 12

Private Tenancies in Scotland

The law governing the relationship between private landlords and tenants in Scotland is different to that in England. Since the beginning of 1989, new private sector tenancies in Scotland were covered by the Housing (Scotland) Act 1988. Following the passage of this Act, private sector tenants no longer had any protection as far as rent levels were concerned and tenants enjoyed less security of tenure. However, **The Private Housing (Tenancies) (Scotland) Act 2016**, passed by the Scottish Parliament and coming into force on 1st December 2017 has changed the law concerning private tenancies in Scotland. The main provisions of the Act are outlined below.

The new Private Residential Tenancy

On 1 December 2017 a new type of tenancy came into force, called the private residential tenancy, it replaced assured and short assured tenancy agreements for all new tenancies from 1st December 2017. as a result of passing of The Private Housing (Tenancies) (Scotland) Act 2016. The new Scottish Private Residential Tenancy, (SPRT) will deliver improved security of tenure for tenants, including students in smaller purpose built and mainstream private rented accommodation, and also the power for local authorities to designate rent pressure zones within their jurisdiction. There will also be streamlined procedures for starting and ending a tenancy and a model agreement for landlords and tenants.

The SPRT will become the standard tenancy agreement between residential landlords and tenants and will replace the most common types of residential tenancies in Scotland – the Short Assured Tenancy and the Assured Tenancy.

What changes has the private residential tenancy brought in?

Any tenancy that started on or after 1 December 2017 will be a private residential tenancy. These new tenancies will bring in changes and improvements to the private rented sector, including:

No more fixed terms - private residential tenancies are open ended, meaning a landlord can't ask a tenant to leave just because they have been in the property for 6 months as they can with a short assured tenancy.

Rent increases – a tenant's rent can only be increased once every 12 months (with 3 months notice) and if they think the proposed increase is unfair they can refer it to a rent officer.

Longer notice period - if a tenant has lived in a property for longer than 6 months the landlord will have to give them at least 84 days notice to leave (unless they have broken a term in the tenancy).

Simpler notices - the notice to quit process has been scrapped and replaced by a simpler notice to leave process.

Model tenancy agreement - the Scottish Government have published a model private residential tenancy that can be used by landlords to set up a tenancy.

Person already an assured/short assured tenant

If a tenant was already renting and were an assured or short assured tenant, on 1 December 2017, their tenancy will continue as normal until they or their landlord brings it to an end following the correct procedure. If a landlord then offers a tenant a new tenancy this will be a private residential tenancy.

What is a private residential tenancy?

A private residential tenancy is one that meets the following conditions:

* the tenancy started on or after 1 December 2017
* it is let to a person as a separate dwelling (home)
* the person must be an individual, meaning not a company
* it's their main or only home
* they must have a lease (although a written agreement not needed for a lease to exist)
* the tenancy is not a exemptions tenancy, as listed below.

Tenancy agreements

A person have the right to a tenancy agreement, which can be either a written or electronic copy, within 28 days of the start of the tenancy. The Scottish Government has published a model tenancy that a landlord can use to set up a tenancy. This tenancy plus a set of notes that a landlord must give to the tenant can be accessed at www.mygov.scot/tenancy-agreement-scotland.

This tenancy agreement contains certain statutory terms that outline both parties rights and obligations including:

* The tenant's and landlord/letting agent's contact details
* The address and details of the rented property
* The start date of the tenancy
* How much the rent is and how it can be increased

117

- How much the deposit is and information about how it will be registered
- Who is responsible for insuring the property.
- The tenant has to inform the landlord when they are going to be absent from the property for more than 14 days
- The tenant will take reasonable care of the property
- The condition that the landlord must make sure the property is in, including the repairing standard.
- That the tenant must inform the landlord the need of any repairs.
- That the tenant will give reasonable access to the property, when the landlord has given at least 48 hours notice

The process that the tenancy can be brought to an end

If a landlord uses the Scottish Government's' model tenancy they should also give the tenant the 'Easy Read Notes' which will explain the tenancy terms in plain English. If a landlord does not use the model tenancy they must give the tenant the private residential tenancy statutory terms: supporting notes, with their lease, which will explains the basic set of terms that a landlord has to include in the lease.

Rent Increases

The rent can only be increase once every 12 months and the landlord needs to give a tenant 3 months notice, using the correct notice of the rent increase. If the tenant doesn't agree to the rent increase they can refer it to the local rent officer. The referral to the rent officer must be done within 21 days of receiving the rent increase notice.

When a referral made to the rent officer, they will first issue a provisional order which will suggest the amount the rent can be increased.

The tenant will have 14 days from the date the provisional order is issued to request a reconsideration. If the tenant requests a reconsideration the rent officer will look at it again before making a final order and telling them the date that the increase will take place.

Ending a tenancy

If a tenant wants to end the tenancy, then they will have to give the landlord 28 days notice in writing. The notice has to state the day on which the tenancy is to end, normally the day after notice period has expired.

The tenant can agree a different notice period with the landlord as long it is in writing. If there is no agreed notice then 28 days notice is the minimum required.

Landlord access

The tenant has to allow reasonable access to the landlord to carry out repairs, inspections, or valuations when:

* the landlord has given at least 48 hours' written notice, or
* access is required urgently for the landlord to view or carry out works in relation to the repairing standard

If a tenant refuses access the landlord can make an application to the First Tier Tribunal Housing and Property Chamber who may make an order allowing them access.

Getting repairs carried out

As with other tenancies, the landlord has to keep the property wind and watertight, and in a condition that is safe to live in. The landlord is also responsible for making sure that the property repairing standard is met. This is a basic level of repair that is required by law. The landlord must give the tenant information on the repairing standard and what they can do if the property does not meet it. If a tenant wants to carry out work on their home, such as redecorating or installing a second phone line, they will need to seek permission from the landlord. Some tenancy agreements will include a clause telling the tenant whether they can carry out this kind of work.

Can a tenant sublet or pass their tenancy on to someone else?
A tenant cannot sublet, take in a lodger or pass their tenancy on to someone else before first getting written agreement from the landlord.

Tenancies that cannot be private residential tenancy
Almost all new private tenancies created on or after 1st December 2017 will be private residential tenancies. However, there are a number of exemptions, including the following:

- Tenancies at a low rent
- Tenancies of shops
- Licensed premises
- Tenancies of agricultural land
- Lettings to students (meaning purpose built student accommodation)
- Holiday lettings
- Resident landlords
- Police Housing
- Military Housing
- Social Housing
- Sublet, assigned etc. social housing
- Homeless persons

- Persons on probation or released from prison etc.
- Accommodation for asylum seekers
- Displaced persons
- Shared ownership
- Tenancies under previous legislation
- Assured or short assured tenancies

Short assured and assured tenancies

Most residential lettings in Scotland made after 2 January 1989 and before 1st December 2017 are short assured tenancies. Those that aren't short assured are normally assured tenancies.

Short assured tenancies

This was the most common type of tenancy. A short assured tenancy makes it easier for a landlord to get a property than an assured tenancy. Before any agreement is signed, a landlord must use form AT5 to tell new tenants that the tenancy will be a short assured tenancy. (see appendix). If they don't, the tenancy will automatically be an assured tenancy. Initially, a short assured tenancy must be for 6 months or more. After the first 6 months, the tenancy can be renewed for a shorter period.

Assured tenancies

At the beginning of an assured tenancy, it will be classed as a 'contractual assured tenancy' for a fixed period of time. The tenancy automatically becomes a 'statutory assured tenancy' if:

- the landlord ends the tenancy by issuing a notice to quit (eg because they want to change the agreement) and the tenant stays in the property

- the fixed period covered by the tenancy comes to an end and the tenant stays in the property

There are different rights and responsibilities on both landlord and tenant depending on the type of assured tenancy.

Other types of tenancy

Most tenancies in Scotland issued before December 2017 are short assured or assured tenancies. The other tenancy types are:

- 'common law' tenancy - if a tenant shares their home as a lodger
- regulated tenancy - the most common form of tenancy before 1989
- agricultural tenancy
- crofting tenancy

'Common law' tenancies

If a landlord is sharing their house or flat with their tenants, they can't use the short assured or assured tenancy. Instead, they will automatically have what is known as a 'common law tenancy'. The tenant doesn't have to have a written contract but the landlord may use a lodger agreement to create a contract between them and the tenant - so both are clear about what has been agreed. (see appendix for sample lodger agreement).

Regulated tenancies

Tenancies created before 2 January 1989 are generally regulated tenancies. As not many exist we will not be describing them further here.

Agricultural tenancies

There are 3 types of agricultural tenancy:

- limited duration tenancy - if the lease is for more than 5 years
- short limited duration tenancy - if the lease is for 5 years or less
- 1991 Act tenancy - if the tenancy began before 2003

All agricultural tenants have the right to:

- a written lease
- compensation at the end of the tenancy for any improvements they made to the land during their tenancy
- leave the tenancy to a spouse or relative in their will

If the lease is over 5 years, agricultural tenants can also:

- pass their tenancy on to a relative or spouse within their lifetime
- use the land for non-agricultural purposes
- Tenants with a 1991 Act tenancy have the right to buy the land they are leasing.

If there's a house on the land, both landlord and tenant have obligations to keep it in good repair.

Crofting tenancies

Crofting is a system of landholding unique to the Highlands and Islands of Scotland. Usually, the crofter holds the croft on the 'statutory conditions' and doesn't have a written lease. Crofting is regulated by the Crofting Commission. The tenant must get written agreement from the Commission if you want to make any changes to a crofting tenancy (including a change of tenant).

What the landlord must include in a tenancy agreement

If a landlord used an assured or short assured tenancy, the agreement must be written down. It must include:

- the names of all people involved
- the rental price and how it's paid
- the deposit amount and how it will be protected (see below)
- when the deposit can be fully or partly withheld (eg to repair damage caused by tenants)
- the property address
- the start and end date of the tenancy
- any tenant or landlord obligations
- who's responsible for minor repairs
- which bills your tenants are responsible for
- a statement telling the tenant that antisocial behaviour is a breach of the agreement

For other types of tenancy, it's still good practice to put the agreement in writing. including other information To avoid any confusion later, the landlord can include other information in the agreement, such as:

- whether the tenancy can be ended early and how this can be done
- information on how and when the rent will be reviewed
- whether the property can be let to someone else (sublet) or have lodgers

Changes to tenancy agreements

The landlord must get the agreement of their tenants if they want to make changes to the terms of their tenancy agreement.

Preventing discrimination

Unless the landlord have a very strong reason, they must change anything in a tenancy agreement that might discriminate against tenants on the grounds of:

* gender
* sexual orientation
* disability (or because of something connected with their disability)
* religion or belief
* being a transsexual person
* the tenant being pregnant or having a baby

Ending a Short assured tenancy

To get a property back, the landlord must give tenants a 'notice to quit' and a 'Section 33 notice'. For a short assured tenancy, the minimum notice period is 40 days if the tenancy is for 6 months or longer.

For a tenancy that is continuing on a month by month basis after the original period has ended, the notice period is a minimum of 28 days. The landlord must give 2 months notice when giving a Section 33 notice. They can issue both the notice to quit and Section 33 notice at the same time. (see appendix)

Other tenancy types (excluding the new private residential tenancy)

For other tenancy types the landlord must give at least:

* 28 days if the tenancy is for up to 1 month
* 31 days if the tenancy is for up to 3 months
* 40 days if the tenancy is for more than 3 months

Ending a tenancy early

A landlord can end a tenancy early if:

* the tenant breaks a condition of the tenancy agreement
* landlord and tenant agree to end the tenancy

If tenants don't leave

If the notice period expires and tenants don't leave the property, the landlord can start the process of eviction through the courts. A landlord must tell tenants of their intention to get a court order by giving them a 'notice of intention to raise proceedings' (AT6) (see appendix).

If tenants want to leave

The tenancy agreement should say how much notice tenants need to give before they can leave the property.

If the notice isn't mentioned in the tenancy agreement, the minimum notice a tenant can give is:

* 28 days if their tenancy runs on a month-to-month basis (or if it's for less than a month)
* 40 days if their tenancy is for longer than 3 months

Ending a tenancy early

Unless there's a break clause in the tenancy agreement, a landlord can insist that their tenants pay rent until the end of the tenancy. If tenants leave the property without giving notice, or before the notice has run out, they're still responsible for the property and the rent by law.

Houses in multiple occupation (HMOs)

If a tenant is living in a bedsit, shared flat, lodging, shared house, hostel or bed and breakfast accommodation it's likely that they will be living a house in multiple occupation or 'HMO'. A landlord will have an HMO if:

* tenants live with two or more other people, and
* they don't belong to the same family, and
* they share some facilities, e.g. a bathroom or kitchen, and
* the accommodation is their only or main home (if they are a student, their term-time residence counts as their main home).

If they live with a homeowner their family doesnt count as 'qualifying persons' when deciding whether or not a property is an HMO. So for example, if they share accommodation with the owner and one other unrelated lodger, they won't live in an HMO. If they live with the owner and two other unrelated lodgers, they will live in an HMO. Before the council gives a landlord an HMO licence, it will carry out the following checks:

Is the landlord a fit and proper person to hold a licence?

Before it will grant an HMO licence, the council must check that the owner and anyone who manages the property (for example, a letting agent) don't have any criminal convictions, for example, for fraud or theft.

Is the property managed properly?

The council must check that the landlord respects tenants legal rights. They should be given a written tenancy agreement stating clearly what the landlord's responsibilities are, and what the tenants responsibilities are.

127

This should cover things like rent, repairs and other rules. To manage the property properly, the landlord must:

- keep the property and any furniture and fittings in good repair
- deal with the tenant fairly and legally when it comes to rent and other payments, for example they:
- must go through the correct procedure if they want to increase the rent
- cannot resell the tenant gas or electricity at a profit
- not evict the tenant illegally
- make sure that their tenants don't annoy or upset other people living in the area.

Does the property meet the required standards?

To meet the standards expected of an HMO property:

- the rooms must be a decent size, for example, every bedroom should be able to accommodate a bed, a wardrobe and a chest of drawers.
- there must be enough kitchen and bathroom facilities for the number of people living in the property, with adequate hot and cold water supplies.
- adequate fire safety measures must be installed, for example the landlord must provide smoke alarms and self-closing fire doors and make sure there is an emergency escape route.
- all gas and electrical appliances must be safe.
- heating, lighting and ventilation must all be adequate.
- the property should be secure, with good locks on the doors and windows.
- there must be a phone line installed so that tenants can set up a contract with a phone company to supply the service.

What are the landlord's responsibilities?

In order to keep their HMO licence, a landlord must maintain the property properly:

Common parts - these must be kept clean and in good repair (for example, the stairwell, hall, shared kitchen and bathroom). However, the landlord can include a clause in the tenancy agreement which passes this responsibility onto the tenants.

Shared facilities - these should be kept in good repair (for example, the cooker, boiler, fridge, sinks, bath and lighting)

Heating, hot water and ventilation - these facilities must all be kept in good order

Gas safety - all gas appliances and installations must be safe (for example, a gas fire, boiler or cooker) - these should be checked once a year by a Gas Safe Register engineer

Electrical safety - all electrical appliances and installations must be safe - these should be tested every three years by a contractor approved by the National Inspection Council for Electrical Installation Contracting (NICEIC) or SELECT, Scotland's trade association for the electrical, electronics and communications systems industry

Fire precautions - all fire precautions (for example, smoke alarms and fire extinguishers) must be in good working order and that the fire escape route is kept safe and free from obstructions

Furniture - all furniture supplied must meet safety standards (for example, isn't flammable)

Roof, windows and exterior - these must all be adequately maintained

Rubbish - enough rubbish bins must be provided

Deposits - tenants deposits must be returned within a reasonable time when they move out, preferably within 14 days.

The landlord should also put up notices in the accommodation:
giving the name and address of the person responsible for managing it so that the tenant can contact them whenever necessary
explaining what the tenant should do in an emergency, for example if there is a gas leak or a fire.

Tenants responsibilities:

Repairs – the tenant should let the landlord know if anything in the property needs repairing, particularly if this is something they are responsible for keeping in good order, such as the roof, boiler or toilet

Damage – the tenant must take good care of the property and try not to damage anything

Rubbish - not let rubbish pile up in or around the property but dispose of it properly in the bins provided

Inspections - let the landlord inspect the property so they can check whether any maintenance work needs doing. Normally this should happen once every six months. The landlord must give you 24 hours' written notice before coming round.

Behave responsibly - make sure that the tenant doesnt behave in a way that can annoy or upset neighbours. The landlord is responsible for dealing with any complaints made by neighbours and must take action if they are unhappy with tenants behaviour.

Safeguarding Tenancy Deposits

A tenancy deposit scheme is a scheme provided by an independent third party to protect deposits until they are due to be repaid. Three schemes are now operating:

Letting Protection Service Scotland
Safedeposits Scotland
Mydeposits Scotland

Landlord's legal duties

The legal duties on landlords who receive a tenancy deposit are:

* to pay deposits to an approved tenancy deposit scheme
* to provide the tenant with key information about the tenancy and deposit

Key dates for landlords

The dates by which landlords must pay deposits to an approved scheme and provide information to the tenant vary, depending on when the deposit was received:

1. Deposit received prior to 7 March 2011:

Where the tenancy is renewed by express agreement or tacit relocation on or after 2 October 2012 and before 2 April 2013 (Regulation 47(a))

Within 30 working days of renewal. In any other case by 15 May 2013

2. Deposit received on or after 7 March 2011 and before 2 July 2012

By 13 November 2012

3. Deposit received on or after 2 July 2012 and before 2 October 2012

By 13 November 2012

4. Deposit received on or after 2 October 2012

Within 30 working days of the beginning of the tenancy

Information about the schemes

Further details about the individual schemes are available on the individual scheme web sites below. Email addresses and telephone numbers are also included. All three schemes have a range of information available for both landlords (and their agents) as well as tenants and these include how landlords can join the schemes, how to submit deposits, how to ask for repayment of deposits and how the dispute resolution service will work.

Letting Protection Service Scotland

www.lettingprotectionscotland.com

Address:

The Pavilions

Bridgwater Road

Bristol

BS99 6BN

Email contact: events@lettingprotectionscotland.com

Telephone: 0330 303 0031

SafeDeposits Scotland

www.safedepositsscotland.com

Address:

Lower Ground

250 West George Street

Glasgow

G2 4QY

Email contact: info@safedepositsscotland.com

Telephone: 03333 213 136

Mydeposits Scotland

www.mydepositsscotland.co.uk

Address:

Premiere House
Elstree Way Borehamwood
Hertfordshire
WD6 1JH
Email contact: info@mydepositsscotland.co.uk
Telephone: 0333 321 9402

**

Ch. 13

Relationship Breakdown and Housing Rights

When a relationship breaks down, whether the people in question are married or not, problems can often occur in relation to the property that was home. The rights of people will depend mainly on whether they are married or not, whether they are in a civil partnership or whether there are children involved and the legal status of individuals in the home.

Housing rights in an emergency

In the main, it is women who suffer from domestic violence. This section refers to women but the rights are the same for men. If you are a woman, and have been threatened by a man and are forced to leave your home then there are several possibilities for action in an emergency. The first of these is either going to a women's refuge. These provide shelter, advice and emotional support for women and children. These refuges will always try to admit you and as a result are sometimes crowded. They will always try to find you somewhere to live in the longer term. Refuges have a 24-hour telephone service if you need to find somewhere. For addresses see *useful addresses* at the back of this book.

Approaching the council

A person suffering domestic violence who has been forced to flee can approach the local council and ask for help as a homeless person. Councils will demand proof of violence and you will need to get evidence from a professional person, such as doctor or social worker or police. The council decides whether or not it has a duty to help you and you should seek advice if they refuse. Some councils, but not all will offer help to battered women. If you are accepted as homeless then the council should not send you back to the area where the violence began.

Obtaining a court order

Another course of action in an emergency is to obtain a court order against the man you live with.

Courts can issue orders stating that a man:

- should not assault you or harass you
- not to assault any children living with you
- to leave the home and not to return
- to keep a certain distance from your home or any other place where your children go regularly.
- to let you back in your home if you have been excluded.

If you believe a court order would help, you should get advice on where to find a solicitor or law centre that deals with these types of applications to the court. Certain orders are harder to get than others, such as exclusion orders. Matters need to be very serious indeed before such an order will be made. However, you will be advised of this when approaching a solicitor or law centre. Failure to obey the terms and conditions laid down in the order can lead to arrest for contempt and a fine or even imprisonment.

Long-term rights to the home

Long-term rights to stay in a home depend on a number of circumstances. If you are married or in a civil partnership and the ownership or tenancy of the property is in joint names you have equal rights to live in the property. If it is owned then you will have a right to a share of the proceeds if it is sold. In certain circumstances you have a right to more (or less) than a half share, or to the tenancy in your name after divorce.

If you are married or in a civil partnership but the ownership or tenancy is in one name only there are laws to protect the rights of the other party. Courts have the power to decide who has the ownership or rights over the matrimonial home, even if the property is held in one persons name only. This can also apply to people who were married but are now divorced and to those who were planning to get married within three years of their engagement.

Spouses who are not the owner or tenant of the home have a right to stay there. The court has the power to exclude either of the spouses, even if they are sole or joint owner or tenant. If your husband has left and stopped paying the rent or mortgage payments, the landlord or building society is obliged to accept payments from you, if you wish to make them, even if the property is not in your name. If the home is owned by your husband then you can register your right to live in it. This prevents your husband selling the home before the court has decided who should live there. And also prevents him taking out a second mortgage on the property without your knowledge. This is known as 'registering a charge' on the home. The court also has the power to transfer a fully protected private tenancy, an assured tenancy or a council or housing association tenancy from one partner to another.

If the matrimonial home is owner occupied and proceedings have started for a divorce, the court will decide how the value of the property will be divided up. The law recognises that, even if the property is in the husbands/civil partners name only, the wife/civil partner has a right to a share in its value, that she/he often makes a large unpaid contribution through housework or looking after children and that this should be recognised in divorce proceedings. The court looks at a number of things when reaching a decision:

- the income and resources of both partners
- the needs of you and your husband
- the standard of living that you and your husband had before the breakdown
- ages of partners and length of marriage/civil partnership
- contributions to the welfare of the family
- conduct of partners
- loss of benefits that you might have had if the marriage/civil partnership had not broken down.

The court also has to consider whether there is any way that they can make a 'clean break' between you and your husband/civil partner so that there are no further financial ties between you. In certain circumstances, the court can order sale of the matrimonial home and the distribution of proceeds between partners.

If you are not married or in a Civil Partnership

If you are not married/in a civil partnership then your rights will depend on who is the tenant or the owner of the home.

Tenants

If a tenancy is in joint names then you both have equal rights to the home. You can exclude your partner temporarily as we have seen by a court order. If you are a council tenant then you may want to see if you can get the council to rehouse you. You should get advice on this from an independent agency (see useful addresses).

If the tenancy is in your partners name only then the other person can apply for the right to stay there, for their partner to be excluded or for the tenancy to be transferred.

Home owners

If you live in an owner occupied property you and you partner may have certain rights to a share of the property even if you are not married/in a civil partnership.

If the home is jointly owned then you have a clear right to a share in its value. If one person has contributed more than the other then a court can decide that an equal share is unfair. The court cannot order the transfer of the ownership of property but it can order the sale and distribution of the proceeds.

If the home is in one persons name there is no automatic right to live in the home, even if there are children. However, a solicitor acting on your behalf can argue that by virtue of marriage/civil partnership and contribution you should be allowed to stay there and be entitled to a share.

**

Ch. 14

Housing Advice

General advice

Citizens Advice Bureaus, which are situated throughout the U.K., provide advice on all problems, including housing and other matters such as legal, welfare benefits and relationship breakdown. If appropriate they can refer you for more specialist help to a solicitor or advice agency. This advice is free of charge. To find a local office, look in the telephone directory under National Association of Citizens Advice Bureau.

Housing Advice Centres

In many areas there are specialist advice centres offering housing aid and advice. The service they offer varies from one-off information to detailed help over a long period.

There are two main types of housing advice centres, Local council housing aid centres which can advise on all kinds of problems, although they will not be able to take action against their own council. Independent housing aid centres may be better equipped to do this. These centres can offer detailed assistance over a length of time and also one-off advice. There are a number of independent housing aid centres throughout the country operated by Shelter. You should contact Shelter for your nearest centre.

139

Other specialist advice

Law centers-they offer free advice and can sometimes represent you in court. They can usually advise on all aspects of law and also advise battered women. They cannot, however, take divorce cases. For this you will need a solicitor. Shelter can provide a list of law centers.

For advice on welfare rights you should try the local council, who may employ a welfare rights advisor. Advisers can also contact the advice line which is run by the Child Poverty Action Group.

For women's rights the Women's Aid Federation England and Welsh Women's Aid refer battered women, with or without children, to refuges. They can put you in touch with sympathetic solicitors and local women's aid groups and can offer a range of other advice, such as welfare benefits.

For immigration advice, the Joint Council for the Welfare of Immigrants offers advice on all types of problems connected with immigration and nationality.

The United Kingdom Immigrants Advisory Service offers advice and help on problems with immigration. The Refugee Council has an advice service for refugees and asylum seekers.

Advice from solicitors

Solicitors can advise you on all aspects of the law, represent you in certain courts and, if necessary, get a barrister to represent you. It is best to find a solicitor who specialises in housing rights as they usually have a wider knowledge of specific areas. You can get a list of solicitors who specialise in housing law from the Community Legal Service (CLS) Directory in your local library. The list is also on the CLS website. Citizens Advice Bureaus can also supply specialist solicitor details.

140

Free advice and help

The Legal Help Scheme, whilst also being squeezed, can pay for up to two hours worth of free advice and assistance and for matrimonial cases up to three hours. The scheme is means tested and you must come within the limits of the scheme to qualify. For details of the scheme you should approach a Citizens Advice Bureau or a solicitors practice operating the scheme. You must have reasonable grounds for defending an action. In certain cases, if you succeed in obtaining cash compensation then you may have to pay a proportion of it back, this is known as the *statutory charge*

**

Ch. 15

Agricultural Tenancies

If a person rents agricultural land or buildings to run a farm business they may have an agricultural tenancy agreement. Every agricultural tenancy agreement is unique. We refer here to 2 types of agricultural tenancies governed by legislation:

• Farm Business Tenancies governed by the Agricultural Tenancies Act 1995 - those agreed after 1 September 1995

• 1986 Act Tenancies governed by the Agricultural Holdings Act 1986 - those agreed before 1 September 1995

Farm Business Tenancies

A tenancy is a Farm Business Tenancy if at least part of the tenanted land is farmed throughout the life of the tenancy. The tenancy must also meet one of these 2 conditions:

• if the tenancy is primarily agricultural to start with, the landlord and tenant can exchange notices before the tenancy begins confirming they intend it to remain a Farm Business Tenancy throughout - this lets tenants diversify away from agriculture where the terms of the tenancy agreement allow this.

- if the landlord and tenant don't exchange notices before the tenancy begins, the tenancy business must be primarily agricultural to be considered a Farm Business Tenancy

Farm Business Tenancy rent reviews

Landlords and tenants can negotiate their own rent levels and decide whether or not they want to have rent reviews. Either the landlord or tenant can demand a rent review every 3 years by law.

However, landlords and tenants can agree on how often a rent review should take place – this agreement replaces the law. For example, tenants can agree on a rent review every 4 years.

Farm Business Tenancy compensation

As a farm business tenant a person is entitled to compensation at the end of a tenancy for:

- physical improvements they made to a holding (provided the landlord has given consent to the improvements)
- changes that increase the value of the holding (provided they are left behind when the tenant leaves)

Owners can agree in writing an upper limit on the amount of compensation, usually equal to the tenant's cost in making the improvements.

Ending a Farm Business Tenancy

Landlords and tenants of a Farm Business Tenancy can end the tenancy by issuing a notice to quit. The minimum notice period to quit is 12 months.

1986 Act agricultural tenancies

Agricultural tenancies agreed before 1 September 1995 are known as 1986 Act Tenancies. They're also sometimes referred to as Full Agricultural Tenancies (FATs) or Agricultural Holdings Act tenancies (AHAs).

These tenancies usually have lifetime security of tenure and those granted before 12 July 1984 also carry statutory succession rights, on death or retirement. This means a close relative of a deceased tenant can apply for succession to the tenancy within 3 months of the tenant's death.

Applying for succession stops any notice to quit given by the landlord on the tenant's death. Two tenancies by succession can be granted, so it's possible for the tenant's family to work the holding for 3 generations. Farmers with a tenancy granted before 12 July 1984 can also name an eligible successor such as a close relative who can apply to take over the holding when they retire.

1986 Act Tenancies rent reviews

The landlord or tenant has the right to a rent review 3 years after either the:

- start of a tenancy
- previous rent review

If land is added to or removed from a holding then the next rent review must be either at least 3 years from one of the following:

- the date the original tenancy began
- from the date of the previous rent review for the original tenancy

This rent review must happen even if the rent has changed to reflect changes to the amount of land on the holding.

1986 Act Tenancies compensation

Under the 1986 Act Tenancy agreements the tenant is entitled to compensation at the end of their tenancy for the following:

- major long-term improvements
- short-term improvements
- 'tenant right'

Major long-term improvements

These include:

- making or planting water meadows
- planting orchards
- erecting or altering buildings
- constructing silos, roads or bridges
- repairs to fixed equipment

Short-term improvements

These include:

- mole drainage
- protecting fruit trees against animals
- clay burning
- liming and chalking of land
- applying manure, fertiliser, soil improvers and digestate to the land (in England)

'Tenant right'

These include:

- the value of growing crops

- the costs of husbandry, such as sowing seeds and cultivations
- compensation for disturbance where a landlord terminates the tenancy with a notice to quit

The amount of compensation is measured by the increase in value to the holding made by the improvements. The landlord may also claim compensation for disrepair - usually the cost of repairing any damage.

Dispute procedures

Where a landlord or a tenant has a dispute relating to an Agricultural Tenancy (either a 1986 Act Tenancy or a Farm Business Tenancy) they can use third-party expert determination or arbitration procedures.

Arbitration is the private legal settlement of a dispute by an independent, professional arbitrator which can involve either of the following:

- a tribunal hearing where both sides present evidence and testimony
- the 2 parties agreeing to resolve the dispute using written arbitration procedures, avoiding the time and costs of a hearing

If a landlord and tenant can't agree on the appointment of an arbitrator, either of them can apply to the President of the Royal Institution of Chartered Surveyors (RICS) to make an appointment on their behalf for an arbitrator to:

- decide a rent review dispute
- resolve a dispute other than a rent review

Contacts

Farmers can get further information on agricultural tenancy issues from the Tenant Farmers Association and the National Farmers Union. Please note that the law differs in Scotland and Wales, information on which can be obtained from these sites.

**

GLOSSARY

FREEHOLDER: Someone who owns their property outright.

LEASEHOLDER: Someone who has been granted permission to live on someone else's land for a fixed term.

TENANCY: One form of lease, the most common types of which are fixed-term or periodic.

LANDLORD: A person who owns the property in which the tenant lives.

LICENCE: A licence is an agreement entered into whereby the landlord is merely giving you permission to occupy his/her property for a limited period of time.

TRESPASSER: Someone who has no right through an agreement to live in a property.

PROTECTED TENANT: In the main, subject to certain exclusions, someone whose tenancy began before 15th January 1989.

ASSURED TENANT: In the main, subject to certain exclusions, someone whose tenancy began after 15th January 1989.

NOTICE TO QUIT: A legal document giving the protected tenant twenty eight days notice that the landlord intends to apply for possession of the property to the County Court.

GROUND FOR POSSESSION: One of the stated reasons for which the landlord can apply for possession of the property.

MANDATORY GROUND: Where the judge must give possession of the property.

DISCRETIONARY GROUND: Where the judge may or may not give possession, depending on his own opinion.

STUDENT LETTING: A tenancy granted by a specified educational institution.

HOLIDAY LETTING: A dwelling used for holiday purposes only.

ASSURED SHORTHOLD TENANCY: A fixed-term post-1989 tenancy.

PAYMENT OF RENT: Where you pay a regular sum of money in return for permission to occupy a property or land for a specified period of time.

FAIR RENT: A rent set by the Rent Officer every two years for most pre-1989 tenancies and which is lower than a market rent.

MARKET RENT: A rent deemed to be comparable with other non-fair rents in the area.

RENT ASSESSMENT COMMITTEE: A committee set up to review rents set by either the Rent Officer or the landlord.

PREMIUM: A sum of money charged for permission to live in a property.

DEPOSIT: A sum of money held against the possibility of damage to property.

QUIET ENJOYMENT: The right to live peacefully in your own Home.

REPAIRS: Work required to keep a property in good order.

IMPROVEMENTS: Alterations to a property.

LEGAL AID: Help with your legal costs, which is dependent on income.

HOUSING BENEFIT: Financial help with rent, which is dependent on income.

HOUSING ADVICE CENTRE: A center which exists to give advice on housing-related matters and which is usually local authority-funded.

LAW CENTRE: A center, which exists for the purpose of assisting the public with legal advice.

**

Appendix 1 - Useful addresses

Age UK
Tavis House
1-6 Tavistock Square
London WC1 9NA
020 7239 0400
www.ageuk.org.uk

Child Poverty Action Group
30 Micawber Street
London N1 7TB
020 7837 7979

Consumers Association
2 Marylebone Road
London NW1 4DF
01992 822 800
www.which.co.uk

Disability Rights UK www.disabiliyrights.org
Plexal
14 East Bay Lane
Here East
Queen Elizabeth Olympic Park-
Stratford
London
E20 3BS 0300 995 0400

Gay and Lesbian Switchboard

0300 330 0630

switchboard.lgbt

Homeless Link

Minories House

2-5 Minories

London EC3N 1BJ

020 7840 3340

www.homeless.org.uk

Immigration Advisory Service

iasservices.org

Generation Rent

Unit E03, The Biscuit Factory,

100 Clements Road,

London SE16 4DG

www.generationrent.org

Leasehold Advisory Service

0207 832 2500

www.lease-advice.org.uk

Legal Action Group

48 Chancery Lane

London

WC2A   1JF

020 7833 2931

www.lag.org.uk

Liberty (Council for Civil Liberties)

Liberty House,

26-30 Strutton Ground,

London, SW1P 2HR

0207 403 3888

www.liberty-humanrights.org.uk

Shelter

Housing and Homeless Charity

0808 800 4444 (advice helpline)

www.england.shelter.org.uk

Will direct you to Shelter Scotland and Shelter Northern Ireland

Women's Aid Federation Helpline

0808 2000 247

www.womensaid.org.uk

**

Appendix

Sample Assured Shorthold Tenancy Agreement (England and Wales)

Sample Section 21 Notice Requiring possession (FORM 6A)

**

ASSURED SHORTHOLD TENANCY AGREEMENT ENGLAND AND WALES

This Tenancy Agreement is between

Name and address of Landlord-

-AND

Name of tenant:

(in the case of Joint Tenants the term "Tenant" applies to each of them and the names of all Joint Tenants should be written above. Each Tenant individually has the full responsibilities and rights set out in this Agreement)

Address-in respect of:

("the Premises")

Description of Premises
-Which comprises of:
Term-The Tenancy is granted for a fixed term of [6] months

Date of start of tenancy-The Tenancy begins on:

("The Commencement Date") and is an assured shorthold monthly tenancy, the terms of which are set out in this Agreement.

Overcrowding-The Tenant agrees not to allow any person other than the Tenant to reside at the Premises.

Payment of Deposit-The Tenant agrees to pay on signing the Agreement a deposit of

£   which will be returnable in full providing that the Landlord may deduct from such sums: The reasonable costs of any necessary repairs to the premises, building or common parts, or the replacement of any or all of the contents where such repair or replacement is due to any act or omission of the Tenant or family or visitors of the Tenant, such sums as are outstanding on leaving the Premises in respect of arrears or other charges including Court costs or other fees.

The deposit will be protected by The Deposit Protection Service (The DPS) in accordance with the Terms and Conditions of The DPS. The Terms and Conditions and ADR Rules governing the protection of the deposit including   the   repayment   process   can   be   found   at www.depositprotection.com

Payment for the premises-
Rent: The rent for the premises is:

Service Charge:
Total:

In this Agreement the term "Rent" refers to the net rent and service charge set out above or as varied from time to time in accordance with this

156

Agreement. The payment of monthly Rent is due in advance on the first Saturday of each month.

The service charge is in respect of the landlord providing the services listed in Schedule 1 to this Agreement for which the Tenant shall pay a service charge to be included in the rent. The service charge may be varied by the landlord in accordance with the terms set out in Schedule 1 to this Agreement.

I/We have read, understood and accept the terms and conditions contained within this agreement which include the standard terms and conditions attached.

Signed by the Tenant

.... Dated:

Signed on behalf of the landlord
.... Dated:

If the Tenant feels that the landlord has broken this Agreement or not performed any obligation contained in it, he/she should first complain to the landlord in writing giving details of the breach or non-performance.

Terms and Conditions

1. It is agreed that:
Changes in Rent-1.1-The landlord may increase or decrease the Rent by giving the Tenant not less than 4 weeks notice in writing of the increase or

decrease. The notice shall specify the Rent proposed. The first increase or decrease shall be on the first day of   following the Commencement Date of this Agreement. Subsequent increases or decreases in the Rent shall take effect on the first day of   in each subsequent year. The revised Rent shall be the amount specified in the notice of increase unless the Tenant exercises his/her right to refer the notice to a Rent Assessment Committee to have a market rent determined in which case the maximum Rent payable for one year after the date specified in the notice shall be the Rent so determined.

Altering the Agreement-1.2-With the exception of any changes in Rent, this Agreement may only be altered by the agreement in writing of both the Tenant and the landlord.

2. The landlord agrees:

Possession-2.1-To give the Tenant possession of the Premises at the commencement of the Tenancy.

Tenant's Right to Occupy-2.2-Not to interrupt or interfere with the Tenant's right peacefully to occupy the Premises except where:

(i)   access is required to inspect the condition of the Premises or to carry out repairs or other works to the Premises or adjoining property; or

(ii)   a court has given the Association possession by ending the Tenancy.

Repair of Structure and Exterior-2.3-To keep in good repair the structure and exterior of the Premises including:

(i)   drains, gutters and external pipes;

(ii)   the roof;

(iii)   outside wall, outside doors, windowsills, window catches, sash cords and window frames including necessary external painting and decorating;

(iv)   internal walls, floors and ceilings, doors and door frames, door hinges and skirting boards but not including internal painting and decoration;

(v)   plasterwork;

(vi)   chimneys, chimney stacks and flues but not including sweeping;

(vii)   pathways, steps or other means of access;

(viii)   integral garages and stores;

(ix)   boundary walls and fences.

Repair of Installations-2.4-To keep in good repair and working order any installations provided by the landlord for space heating, water heating and sanitation and for the supply of water, gas and electricity including:

(i)   basins, sinks, baths, toilets, flushing systems and waste pipes;

(ii)   electric wiring including sockets and switches, gas pipes and water pipes;

(iii)   water heaters, fireplaces, fitted fires and central heating installations

Repair of Common Parts-2.5-To take reasonable care to keep the common entrances, halls, stairways, lifts, passageways, rubbish chutes and any other common parts, including their lighting, in reasonable repair and fit for use by the Tenant and other occupiers and visitors to the Premises.

External & Internal

Decorations-2.6-To keep the exterior and interior of the Premises and any common parts in a good state of decoration and normally to decorate these areas once every 5 years.

3. The Tenant agrees:

Possession-3.1-To take possession of the Premises at the commencement of the Tenancy and not to part with possession of the Premises or sub-let the whole or part of it.

Rent-3.2-To pay the Rent monthly and in advance. The first payment shall be made on the signing of the Agreement in respect of the period from the Commencement Date to the first Saturday of the following month.

Use of Premises-3.3-To use the Premises for residential purposes as the Tenant's only or principal home and not to operate a business at the Premises without the written consent of the landlord.

Nuisance and Racial and other Harassment-3.4-Not to behave or allow members of his/her household or any other person visiting the Premises with the Tenant's permission to behave in a manner nor do anything which is likely to be a nuisance to the tenants, owners or lessees of any of the other properties or other persons lawfully visiting the property. In particular, not to cause any interference, nuisance or annoyance through noise, anti-social behaviour or threats of or actual violence or any damage to property belonging to the said persons. This Clause also applies to any conduct or activity which amounts to harassment including: abuse and intimidation, creating unacceptable levels of noise or causing intentional damage or any other persistent behaviour which causes offence, discomfort or inconvenience on the grounds of colour, race religion, sex, sexual orientation and disability.

Noise-3.5-Not to play or allow to be played any radio, television, audio equipment or musical instrument so loudly that it causes a nuisance or annoyance to neighbours or can be heard outside the Premises.

Domestic Violence-3.6-Not to use or threaten violence against any other person living in the Premises such that they are forced to leave by reason of the Tenant's violence or fear of such violence.

Pets-3.7-To keep under control any animals at the Premises and to obtain the written consent of the landlord before keeping a dog or any other animal.

Car Repairs-3.8-That no car servicing or car repairs shall be carried out in the roads or accessway or parking spaces or in the forecourt or approaches to the Premises, such as to be a nuisance or annoyance to neighbours.

Paraffin-3.9-Not to use any paraffin or bottled gas heating, lighting or cooking appliances on the Premises nor any appliances which discharge the products of combustion into the interior of the Premises.

Vehicles-3.10-That no commercial vehicle, caravan, boat, or lorry shall be parked in the accessway or parking spaces (regardless of whether this forms part of the Premises) or in the forecourt or approaches to the Premises or the adjoining premises.

Keeping premises clean-3.11-To keep the interior of the Premises in a clean condition. The Tenant agrees to return the property in the same decorative order as at the start of the tenancy taking into account fair wear and tear.

Damage-3.12-To make good any damage caused wilfully or by neglect or carelessness on the part of the Tenant or any member of the Tenant's household or visitor to the Premises including the replacement of any broken glass in windows and repair or replacement of any damaged fittings and installations. If the Tenant fails to make good any damage for which he/she is responsible the landlord may enter the Premises and carry out the work in default and the cost of this work shall be recoverable by the Association from the Tenant.

Reporting Disrepair-3.13-To report to the landlord any disrepair or defect for which the landlord is responsible in the structure or exterior of the Premises or in any installation therein or in the common parts.

Access-3.14-To allow the landlords employees or contractors acting on behalf of the landlord access at all reasonable hours of the daytime to inspect the condition of the Premises or to carry out repairs or other works to the Premises or adjoining property. The landlord will normally give at least 24 hours' notice, but immediate access may be required and shall be given in an emergency.

Assignment-3.15-Not to assign the Tenancy.

Sub-Tenants-3.16-Not to sub-let the whole or part of the Premises.

Ending the Tenancy-3.17-To give the landlord at least [4] weeks notice in writing when the Tenant wishes to end the Tenancy.

Moving Out-3.18-To give the landlord vacant possession and return the keys of the Premises at the end of the Tenancy and to remove all personal possessions and rubbish and leave the Premises and the landlords furniture and fixtures in good lettable condition and repair. The landlord accepts no responsibility for anything left at the Premises by the Tenant at the end of the Tenancy.

4. The Tenant has the following rights:

Right to Occupy-4.1-The Tenant has the right to occupy the Premises without interruption or interference from the landlord for the duration of this Tenancy (except for the obligation contained in this Agreement to give access to the landlords employees or contractors) so long as the Tenant complies with the terms of this Agreement and has proper respect for the rights of other tenants and neighbours.

Security of Tenure-4.2-The Tenant has security of tenure as an assured tenant so long as he/she occupies the Premises as his/her only or principal home. Before the expiry of the fixed term the landlord can only end the Tenancy by obtaining a court order for possession of the Premises on one of the grounds listed in Schedule 2 of the Housing Act 1988. The landlord will only use the following grounds to obtain an order for possession

--The tenant has not paid rent which is due; (Ground 10)

The Tenant has broken, or failed to perform, any of the conditions of this Tenancy; (Ground 12)

The Tenant or anyone living in the premises has caused damage to, or failed to look after the premises, the building, any of the common parts; (Ground 13)

The Tenant or anyone living in the premises has caused serious or persistent nuisance or annoyance to neighbours, or has been responsible for any act of harassment on the grounds of race, colour, religion, sex, sexual orientation, or disability, or has been convicted of using the property for immoral or illegal purposes; (Ground 14) or because of domestic violence (Ground 14A)

Where the tenancy has devolved under the will or intestacy of the Tenant

Suitable alternative accommodation is available to the Tenant

Notice Periods for ending Assured Tenancy-4.3-Before the expiry of the fixed term the landlord agrees that it will not give less than four weeks notice in writing of its intention to seek a possession order except where it is seeking possession on Ground 14 or Ground 14A (whether or not combined with other Grounds) where it shall give such period of notice that it shall decide and that is not less than the statutory minimum notice period

Expiry of Tenancy-4.4-The landlord can only end the Tenancy by giving the Tenant at least two months notice that it requires possession of the Premises and by obtaining a court order for possession. The court will make an order for possession if it is satisfied that the proper notice has been given.

Cessation of Assured Tenancy-4.5-If the Tenancy ceases to be an assured tenancy the landlord may end the Tenancy by giving four weeks' notice in writing which shall be validly served on the Tenant if posted or delivered to the Premises.

**

Department for
Communities and
Local Government

Notice seeking possession of a property let on an Assured Shorthold Tenancy (Form 6a)

This form should be used where a no fault possession of accommodation let under an assured shorthold tenancy (AST) is sought under section 21(1) or (4) of the Housing Act 1988.

This form must be used for all ASTs created on or after 1 October 2015 except for statutory periodic tenancies which have come into being on or after 1 October 2015 at the end of fixed term ASTs created before 1 October 2015.

The validity period of this form is six months following the date of its issue unless the tenancy is a periodic tenancy under which more than two months' notice is required, in which case the validity period is four months from the date the tenant is required to leave (see notes accompanying the form).

You cannot use this form:

> in the first four months of the tenancy (but where the tenancy is a replacement tenancy, the four month period is calculated by reference to the start of the original tenancy and not the start of the replacement tenancy – see section 21(4B) of the Housing Act 1988);
>
> where the landlord is prevented from retaliatory eviction under section 33 of the Deregulation Act 2015;
>
> where the landlord has not provided the prescribed information and/or prescribed documents as set out below;
>
> where the landlord has not complied with the tenancy deposit protection legislation; or
>
> where a property requires a licence but is unlicensed.

Prescribed Information

The landlord is required to provide a copy of the Department for Communities and Local Government's publication "How to rent: the checklist for renting in England" by providing a pdf copy (which may be obtained from www.gov.uk/government/publications/how-to-rent). We recommend that this should be given at the start of the tenancy. Landlords are not required to supply a further copy of the publication each time a different version is published during the tenancy.

Where the landlord has failed to provide the publication, this form may not be used. However, this restriction is lifted as soon as the publication has been provided.

The requirement does not apply where a landlord is a private registered provider of social housing or where a landlord has already provided the tenant with an up-to-date version of the booklet under an earlier tenancy.

If the tenant has not notified the landlord, or a person acting on behalf of the landlord, of an e-mail address at which the tenant is content to accept service of notices and other documents given under or in connection with the tenancy, the landlord must provide a paper copy of the publication.

Prescribed documents:

Where the landlord has failed to comply with certain existing legal obligations, this form may not be used. However, this restriction is lifted as soon as the obligations have been complied with. The obligations are the requirement on a landlord to provide the tenant with:

- an Energy Performance Certificate (Reg 6(5), The Energy Performance of Buildings (England and Wales) Regulations 2012); and

- a gas safety certificate (Reg 36(6)(a), The Gas Safety (Installation and Use) Regulations 1998)

Tenants that need advice about this notice, and what to do about it, should take it immediately to a citizens' advice bureau, a housing advice centre, a law centre or a solicitor.

Tenants can also get expert, independent advice free from Shelterline on 0808 800 4444. Their advisers will be able to give expert advice, independent advice.

**Department for
Communities and
Local Government**

FORM 6A
Notice seeking possession of a property
let on an Assured Shorthold Tenancy

Housing Act 1988 section 21(1) and (4) as amended by section 194 and paragraph 103 of Schedule 11 to the Local Government and Housing Act 1989 and section 98(2) and (3) of the Housing Act 1996

Please write clearly in black ink. Please tick boxes where appropriate.

This form should be used where a no fault possession of accommodation let under an assured shorthold tenancy (AST) is sought under section 21(1) or (4) of the Housing Act 1988.

There are certain circumstances in which the law says that you cannot seek possession against your tenant using section 21 of the Housing Act 1988, in which case you should not use this form. These are:

 (a) during the first four months of the tenancy (but where the tenancy is a replacement tenancy, the four month period is calculated by reference to the start of the original tenancy and not the start of the replacement tenancy – see section 21(4B) of the Housing Act 1988);

 (b) where the landlord is prevented from retaliatory eviction under section 33 of the Deregulation Act 2015;

 (c) where the landlord has not provided the tenant with an energy performance certificate, gas safety certificate or the Department for Communities and Local Government's publication "How to rent: the checklist for renting in England" (see the Assured Shorthold Tenancy Notices and Prescribed Requirements (England) Regulations 2015);

 (d) where the landlord has not complied with the tenancy deposit protection legislation; or

 (e) where a property requires a licence but is unlicensed.

 Landlords who are unsure about whether they are affected by these provisions should seek specialist advice.

This form must be used for all ASTs created on or after 1 October 2015 except for statutory periodic tenancies which have come into being on or after 1 October 2015 at the end of fixed term ASTs created before 1 October 2015. There is no obligation to use this form in relation to ASTs created prior to 1 October 2015, however it may nevertheless be used for all ASTs.

What to do if this notice is served on you

You should read this notice very carefully. It explains that your landlord has started the process to regain possession of the property referred to in section 2 below.

You are entitled to at least two months' notice before being required to give up possession of the property. However, if your tenancy started on a periodic basis without any initial fixed term a longer notice period may be required depending on how often you are required to pay rent (for example, if you pay rent quarterly, you must be given at least three months' notice, or, if you have a periodic tenancy which is half yearly or annual, you must be given at least six months' notice (which is the maximum)). The date you are required to leave should be shown in section 2 below. After this date the landlord can apply to court for a possession order against you.

Where your tenancy is terminated before the end of a period of your tenancy (e.g. where you pay rent in advance on the first of each month and you are required to give up possession in the middle of the month), you may be entitled to repayment of rent from the landlord under section 21C of the Housing Act 1988.

If you need advice about this notice, and what you should do about it, take it immediately to a citizens' advice bureau, a housing advice centre, a law centre or a solicitor.

To:

Name(s) of tenant(s) (Block Capitals)

> [ ]
>
> [ ]

You are required to leave the below address after [   ] [1]. If you do not leave, your landlord may apply to the court for an order under section 21(1) or (4) of the Housing Act 1988 requiring you to give up possession.

Address of premises

> [ ]

Landlords should insert a calendar date here. The date should allow sufficient time to ensure that the notice is properly served on the tenant(s). This will depend on the method of service being used and landlords should check whether the tenancy agreement makes specific provision about service. Where landlords are seeking an order for possession on a periodic tenancy under section 21(4) of the Housing Act 1988, the notice period should also not be shorter than the period of the tenancy (up to a maximum of six months), e.g. where there is a quarterly periodic tenancy, the date should be three months from the date of service.

Form 6A

3. This notice is valid for six months only from the date of issue unless you have a periodic tenancy under which more than two months' notice is required (see notes accompanying this form) in which case the notice is valid for four months only from the date specified in section 2 above.

4. Name and address of landlord

   To be signed and dated by the landlord or their agent (someone acting for them). If there are joint landlords each landlord or the agent should sign unless one signs on behalf of the rest with their agreement.

   Signed

   Date (DD/MM/YYYY)

   Please specify whether: ☐ landlord ☐ joint landlords ☐ landlord's agent

   Name(s) of signatory/signatories (Block Capitals)

   Address(es) of signatory/signatories

   Telephone of signatory/signatories

Index